The Eight Animals of BaGua Zhang
A Martial Practice for Health

Ted Mancuso

Plum Publications
Santa Cruz, California
2013

The Eight Animals of Bagua Zhang

Copyright 2013

First Edition 2013

ISBN: 978-0-9790159-9-1
Printed in the United States of America

Disclaimer
The author and publisher of this book are not responsible for any injury which may result from attempting those movements contained here. Before starting any of the physical activities described, the reader should consult a physician or health provider for advice regarding the suitability of performing these activities.

No part of this publication may be reproduced or transmitted in any form, including electronically, or by any means, without persmission in writing from the author. This notice excepts brief quotations embodied in critical articles and reviews.

Inquiries should be made to the publisher:

Plum Publications
P. O. Box 1134
Santa Cruz, California 95061

www. plumpub.com
shayman@plumpub.com

Table of Contents

v.	The Twisting Place
vii.	How to Circle Through this Book
1	Points on the Circle: Walking Practice
6	The Art of the Legs
8	The Mud Treading Step
11	Turning Around and Changing the Circle

The Animals

23	General Comments on the Animals
30	The Lion Opens His Jaws
42	The Snake Hides in the Grass
52	The Black Bear Turns His Back
62	The Phoenix Glides Through the Air
74	The Eagle Spreads its Wings
86	The Sparrow Hawk Penetrates Heaven
96	The Unicorn Spits the Book
108	The Monkey Offers Fruit
119	The Philosophy of Change
122	Bagua and Qigong
126	The Spirit of Bagua
128	Changing Perspective, Perceiving Change
130	Never too Clearly
132	Bagua Zhang's Animal Techniques
133	Bagua's Nature
136	Questions and Some Answers
141	Biographical Notes

A Twisting Place

When you practice Bagua you have to enter another world. Bagua reminds me of that great book, FLATLAND, by Edwin Abbot. It tells the story of a world entirely composed of a single flat plane. The inhabitants have no 3rd dimension and cannot even conceive of one.

For instance, they may be able to see a point or even a circle but never a ball. They would regard a sphere passing through their plane of existence as a point that widened into a circle then shrank back to a point only to disappear completely.

To do Bagua, really do it, you have to start as soon as possible thinking outside the circle and into the sphere. Everything in Bagua twists. There are no "two-space" moves. Each action may have you twist your arms this way or that. Turn your head. Walk in a circle.

Your normal, erect standing posture will seem supplemented by a torque to one side or the other. Bagua is a little like a car with an alignment issue: when you take your hands off the wheel you start drifting. On the Bagua freeway, this is desirable. It takes a while to fully realize that you now live in Bagua world where this twisting feeling is constant. Eventually you will enjoy this. It is good to remind yourself that the twisting world of Bagua is actually more real than you might suspect. After all, there are few straight lines in the human being. Think about it. All the joints are semi-spherical and most of the muscles have a twist to them even when you relax. Human beings were designed to turn and rotate, not move on a two-dimensional geometric plane. In fact, though you may move your hand or leg seemingly in a straight line, if you watch how your joints actually motivate your movement you will trace everything back to some type of rotation from the generating part of the body.

When most of us were farmers working the soil or hunters prowling the tundra we probably moved far more gracefully and freely. Even the simple act of pulling a root requires some twisting movement. As with so many other tasks, we have been twisting everything from tubers to mayonnaise jars for a thousand years.

But two important changes have occurred in the last few centuries. Industrialization has brought the car and the cubicle into our lives. And we have adapted. People spend hours each day in cubicles often working with tools that demand linear motion. After work, we drop by the gym and work with equipment set up with tracks. We willingly reinforce a robotic type of movement and attitude toward our own bodies. This is perfectly obvious in our manufacturing, as it were, of even feminine beauty curves have been replaced by "being cut." It's a wonder that our bodies haven't begun to evolve into squares.

Another adaptation creates the dominance of vision. Tactility, odor and hearing are devalued survival skills now. Our dominant sense—vision—is by definition a straight line activity. We see in straight lines even if we are squinting through a periscope.

The antidote for all this edgy specialization is a simple, return to a world scaled to human needs. This would not be the first attempt to promote a rounder community. In the Victorian days, William Morris and others promoted the craftsman movement, the artistic correlate of the Pre-Raphaelites. In modern times the great book, "A Pattern Language," is an example of this radical consciousness. If these ideas have merit, shaping the environs we inhabit to more perfectly reflect the organic aspects of human life, then re-programming our bodies can only be another powerful tool for recapturing the non-conforming spirit.

When we enter the circle of Bagua followers we maintain the idea of twisting, spiraling, and drilling as our means of perfecting ourselves. Twisting becomes our default for any situation. My own students have become so accustomed to my "more twist" that they just laugh at how persistently I use the same hammer for so many types of nails.

How to Circle through this Book
This is a book showing you how to acquire a fundamental level of skills and experience in the Chinese martial art known as Bagua Zhang. It might be an obvious assumption that you already know about the martial art called Bagua Zhang, or you would not have gotten your hands on this volume. That sort of speculation aside, I want to talk a moment about this amazing martial art. I will assume you are not a stranger to martial arts, but might not be all that familiar with Bagua Zhang.

Like Tai Chi, Sort of...
Bagua Zhang can be compared to the better known art of Tai Chi Chuan. Both are Chinese and both have origins in the martial heritage. There are definite similarities and differences. The first and most obvious distinguishing feature is that Bagua is typically practiced while walking a circle. On the side of similarities, if you are already familiar with Tai Chi you will recognize some of the rather intricate and beautiful hand positions. You might also see parallels in the slow pace of the formal practice. Many of the benefits of Tai Chi are also available to the Bagua practitioner, because both arts are based on core Chinese concepts such as Yin and Yang, the vital energy known as "qi" and a holistic approach to health and human optimization.

Differences and Similarities:
Each art has unique features that belie any family resemblance. For instance, Tai Chi is often practiced as a medium-to-long choreographed sequence, called a "form," that may require from six to twenty minutes or more to perform.

Bagua, on the other hand, is made up of smaller sequences. In addition, these sequences may be shuffled and practiced in different orders. In fact the entire series need not be practiced each session. The style allows a flexible approach, encouraging you to practice whatever seems appropriate at the moment.

If you are familiar with Qigong, a form of Chinese respiratory exercise, you will find that each art has specific Qigong exercises tailored to it. Both disciplines have partner exercises performed in pairs and ranging from rehearsed, repeated patterns to controlled and gentle sparring. Both have advanced forms utilizing classical weapons. Both are so-called "internal" styles which means, basically, martial and Qigong movements mixed together.

So What is Bagua Anyway?

First, let's get the name right. The full name is Bagua *Zhang* which means Eight Trigrams *Palm*. We always try to add the word Zhang or "palm" because the phrase "Bagua" may be used in Chinese culture for everything from flower arranging to gambling.

Bagua Zhang is a martial art combining profound health practice, performance art, and philosophy all brought together under one roof. It is also an "energetics" practice, meaning it is involved with the Chinese concept of vital energy known as qi, but more of that later.

Bagua Zhang is based firmly on three practices:

1. Walking: You walk in a circle. The size of the circle will vary. Initially the walking will be continuous and casual. As you progress there will be more intricate moves and deeper stances. The advantage of a book like this is that you can choose your rate of progress. Never push to new information until you feel comfortable with what you already practice.

2. Holding: Sometimes you will maintain a certain posture without moving for a few minutes. This comes under the category of Qigong. Other times you will be walking while simultaneously holding your arms and upper body in some fixed position. As you walk around the circle you will constantly adjust to keep your arms fixed.

3. Palm Changing: The third practice involves Palm Changes. These occur when you reverse the direction you are walking on the circle. For instance, if you are walking around the circle counter-clockwise, then perform a Palm Change—a combination of hand and leg actions—Voila! you are now walking in the clockwise direction.

That's it: Walk. Hold. Change. All of Bagua Zhang's other

skills, depending on your interest, practice and talent, will derive in some way from these three modes of movement. It is really kind of wonderful because the core practices never leave you and, no matter how good you become, will always allow you to break your actions into palpable bits.

How to Create Bagua Body
The section you will be reading next is a checklist with an explanation of some goals and regulations. Aspiring to them assures that your Bagua will be the real stuff and will give you the best return for your practice investment.

I have included some background and the reasoning behind the rules to make them easier to understand and, through practice, put into effect. What follows is exactly as you would find in a Chinese martial text, a diagnostic list of the parts of the body and what to do with them. But if you read all this postural stuff right now you will probably close the book, overwhelmed because you have not even taken your first step. So do this: skim this section and then, when you start the real practice, come back and start adding these structural points. I put them first because they are indeed foundational. But the best way to go is to add these ideas slowly and think of them as long term goals. Don't fuss, there's plenty of time.

The Head: Straight and erect.
The bottom line in this art is a circle and that means everything rotates. As you circle you must maintain a vertical axis along your spine, or you are going to tilt, fall, crash and spin out. Can you always retain erect posture when fighting? Of course not. But during practice you can condition yourself to be able to sense the slightest deviation from the vertical. Imagine closely watching a gauge needle to detect lists to one side or the other. In Bagua you want to recognize a balanced position, so you can judge when to give it up or modify it. To aid that straight spine, tuck the chin in a bit, lengthening the cervical vertebrae. Keep your eyes looking straight ahead. The entire upper body should feel somewhat "light" and unrestrained. In other words, do not use tension to keep erect but gently encourage yourself as though you were stacking children's blocks, one atop another.

The Spine:
Almost all of the those Chinese martial practices known as the "Internal" styles favor a slightly tucked pelvis. The Tai Chi phrase for rotating the pelvis—known as "tuck and stack", used long before physical therapists adopted the term, pretty well explains the plan. Bagua is different. It twists and turns. In Bagua Zhang the sensation in the spine is more like gripping the string of a helium filled balloon, a light constant upward pull. Once you have this feeling you should turn slightly toward the direction of the circle's centerpoint. If you are walking counter-clockwise, this will be slightly to the left; if clockwise, then slightly to the right. When walking the circle there will always be a twist aimed one way or the other. As you learn the animals, the skill will be to recognize which twist goes with what animal.

The Knees:
The saying goes that in Bagua Zhang the knees should "support" each other. This means that the knees always act together, as though you were squeezing a pillow or a spongy ball between them as you walked. In most cases the knees should be separated by a distance of less than a 12 inches and kept that way, at least while you walk. Do this enough and you will feel an invisible rubber band connection between them. This is a good sign and testifies that you are using them in concert with one another. Bagua has a lot of stepping patterns (bu fa) that will have your knees aimed at each other. In fact, during these movements you actually will try to touch your knees against one another. There are other stances where you will sit down and really open your legs. In every case, close or wide, the knees feel their mutual attraction. This is not just good practice, it helps protect the knees from doing anything too creative.

The Feet:
    In a perfect Bagua stride the soles of the feet act like magnetic boots. Each step hits the ground, instantly flat. Each step is lifted from the ground with absolutely no roll of the ankle, no peeling of the heel off the earth. To be honest, this is one of the most difficult things to do when practicing Bagua.

This is the Fox Trot, quick-quick-slow, of the martial arts. Or, to put it as my teacher, Adam Hsu, always reminds us, "When you are the Grandmaster of the system, you will still be working on this." Also, try not to let one foot get in the other's way. They will want to cross in front of each other constantly, but imagine each foot has a car lane of its own and stays in it.

The Dizzy Issue
Many of my students started out quite dizzy, then gradually overcame their vertigo. People who have felt this way all their lives often discard that feeling after practicing Bagua, even for a short while The problem is that I cannot tell you the exact method they used because it differed with each person and, very often, utilized a constellation of practices —sometimes unconsciously. I can give you some very intriguing methods to test...

You will discover other odd behaviors, not necessarily dizziness, popping up as you master walking. For instance, you will walk ten perfect circles and, on the eleventh, feel you body rebel with crazy energy almost pitching you out of the circle like the ball in a bingo tumbler. Then there's the fact, at first seemingly normal, that going in one direction feels fine and the other seems completely alien. This makes perfect sense. We each of us have asymmetrical bodies and prejudiced experiences. Even this will not be consistent. You may make the frustrating discovery that the "good" and "bad" sides switch every so often like a magnetic reversal of the Earth's poles, though not nearly so well spaced in time. Practice is the answer for dizziness as well as these other unique reactions. With enough practice racked up— just accepting the strange little quirks—everything will gradually smooth out. You have to go through the practice to be able to practice at your best. I would say it's a bit like a "vicious circle," but that would be, well, a vicious pun.

Points on the Circle

Walking the circle can be a breeze or it can be a truly intense experience that feels like a cross between running an obstacle course and solving calculus problems in your head. As you get swept up in the fascination for this practice, you will probably find yourself ranging the difficulty of your practice all the way from 1 to 10. Walk around a circle a few times and see for yourself.

Practice #1: Walking.

So let's get right to it. Here's how to begin. This tried and true practice emphasizes consistency, but not the kind that makes you into a robot with the task of circling a millstone. Bagua is one of the most un-robotic of all martial arts styles and you don't want to lose this in your practice.

Mark a circle on the ground, floor, deck or dirt. It should be about eight steps in circumference. The best way to do this is to draw two intersecting lines on the X and Y axis. Then draw two more at forty-five degrees. There you have your eight directions. Start at one line and step to the next in rotation. Then step again to the third line. If the step seems too small move further from the centerpoint and try again till your two strides seems natural and not forced. This is the edge of your circle, so mark that.

Now you start. Imagine you are walking the rim of a big clock lying on the ground, face up, and put yourself at 6:00, stepping with your left foot to about 4:30. Then your right foot hits at 3:00, your left at 1:30, your right at 12:00, etc. Just to make he pattern clear, your left will hit at 4:30, 1:30, 10:30 and 7:30 while your right marks 3:00, 12:00, 9:00 AND 6:00. (This clock only has an hour hand so don't try any contorted version of the splits). Each step takes you roughly an eighth of the way around the circle. Simple, and very good for seeing if your stride is consistent.

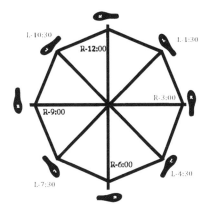

Circling Basics

Eight Step Walking

Bagua often starts with the Eight Step Circle, in part because Ba means "8" in Chinese and each side of the circle represents one of the eight primordial trigrams. Another nice thing about the eight step circle is that it is large enough to accommodate your footwork without causing contortion or pulled muscles, but small enough for you to feel a consistent turning, and thereby gauge the accuracy of your stepping.

While some Bagua practitioners place bricks in the Eight Step (ba bu) pattern and use them to standardize their treads (falling off a brick will definitely tell you the stepping is not quite perfect) I recommend something easier to start with like chalk marks or following a pattern in the floor tiles. Don't worry, there will be plenty of time later to dodge spears and walk on the thin edge of fire pots.

When in Doubt, Just Take a Stroll.

You will have a number of ideas thrown at you: turning steps, scissors actions, inside and outside stepping, mud stepping and more. The best way to approach this is to start each session just walking, as though you were strolling through a garden or taking a sunny walk in the park. Every step you take is practice, so when it all gets too overwhelming just walk the circle and don't worry about the details. The simple truth is that the walking practice is the core of the training.

It literally re-programs your brain. It is what the Chinese monks searched for over centuries; a movement with no corners, as even and unchanging as seated meditation. That is why walking in a manner very similar to this is the basis of certain Daoist sects such as the Black Hat School (famous for their Feng Shui) and the well known walking Zen of Japanese monasteries. While not meditation exactly, taking this approach to the practice can offer immediate benefits, like relaxation for instance.

You have done it. You are now practicing Bagua Zhang. If you get tired of walking in one direction just turn and go the other way for now. Later, you will learn some special ways to make these changes.

Key:
It is traditional to refer to walking in the counter-clockwise direction as the Yin direction and clockwise as the Yang direction. I will continually use the Yin direction, unless I state otherwise, to describe all the animals and Palm Changes. Starting in this same direction each time will eliminate headaches, eye strain and needless confusion.

Ten Step Version
After you've worked with the Eight Step circle, try the Ten Step version. This is actually easier. It makes for interesting footwork, a little different approach. At the half-circle points say 6:00 and 12:00 you will step with opposite feet. If the left treads at 6:00 the right will tread at 12:00. In this case, the outside leg will hit at both cardinal and ordinal directions.

This circle is actually easier as far as rotation of the leg is concerned. The rule is, the bigger the circle the less torque you have to put on the hip and knee joint. This works right up to a great circle encompassing the whole world and looking like a straight line, where there is almost no torque in the legs. Each size circle has its own feel and requirements. Later, you might even try a smaller-than-eight circle. This keeps you guessing.

More About Walking: Start Casually
Just the simple act of walking the circle can be practiced in an amazing number of ways. The act of circling must be so ingrained in the human psyche that we find ourselves doing it over and over, aware of it or not. Lost in the forest, we circle.

Worrying a problem, we circle it mentally, as we do, troubles and joys throughout the length of our lives. You could go on and on, symbolically, but personal experience with this very particular version of circling is what you are really seeking.

Walk around the circle, almost casually at first. Don't even worry about your arms or your steps. Keep your eyes focused on the center. When you begin you may want to put something like a bucket, rock or whatever in the middle of the circle to mark it. Circling a pole is even a better practice because then you won't have to look down and weaken your posture. As you walk you may find you get dizzy. This is only natural. Stop at any point you wish. After all no one is stalking you around the circle—yet.

After circling in this relaxed manner, start to really concentrate and walk an eight or ten step circle, trying to be exact with your steps.

The Yin and Yang of Walking

Chinese philosophy is a kind of code, much like DNA. The basis of this is the binary system of Yin and Yang. In the very early days of Chinese culture these were represented by two symbols: a straight line proxy for Yang, and a broken or double line, standing in for Yin.

Our modern pseudo-pragmatic stance tends to regard everything that isn't irreducibly factual as a metaphor (or worse, a lie). Yin and Yang is not a metaphor. Here are canny observations and profound principles. The single and double line arrangement is derived from some simple ideas. The unbroken line starts as a single event, a single entity alone in the universe. This is the male. The split line represents the female producing a child. This reproduction is fraught with potential, the mitosis that peoples the earth. Early Chinese culture venerated female contributions even if later centuries often suppressed women. For instance, in ancient days the family name of each child was derived through the female clan name. Even today, the Chinese symbol for one's honorable family name is a character combined from that of "woman" and "young plant sprout." In this view Yang represents integration or concentration and Yin represents opening or outward movement.

The Two Biggies: Bai Bu and Kou Bu

One way in which this duality of Yin and Yang presents itself is a Bagua breakthrough. With all the fancy, flying and fighting stepping patterns developed over three thousand years of Kung Fu, Bagua boils them all down to only two, the two basic steps of Bagua: kou bu and bai bu. The basic instructions are simple: In kou bu, you toe in when you step. In bai bu, you toe out. Essentially, that's the whole story. The fact that there are only two stepping patterns really shows how sophisticated Bagua is. Earlier styles created hundreds of years before this art, actually have many forms of stepping. Many Kung Fu forms are distinguished solely by their foot patterns on the floor: tree-shaped, cross-shaped, etc.

The simple twin steps show a basic revelation about footwork as insightful as realizing that there are only three primary colors that make up all the other colors. So you've got it: kou bu means inward. bai bu means outward. But I'm sure you did not think you would get out that easy.

There are a few tiny technical considerations. When you walk the circle your outside leg is always performing a kou bu and your inner leg is always performing a bai bu, both perfectly matching the circle shape. And, you will note at some point, the outer (bai bu) foot is indeed making a slightly larger circle than the inside leg. Don't let the details bother you at this stage; just remember which is which.

The Art of the Legs

Bagua concentrates on the legs. That's nothing new for a martial art. Stances are foundational and proper balance is a must. The practitioner of Chinese martial arts spends more time working on posture and stance than the student of almost any other form of martial studies.

And yet Bagua starts with movement, not stance. Some styles of CMA, such as Hung Ga (Hung Family Boxing) or Baji Quan (Eight Extremes Boxing), use the classical Kung Fu stances as their foundation. But this is not the primary form of practice in Bagua Zhang. No, Bagua Zhang foot training starts with walking and ends with walking.

Bagua Zhang's means of locomotion is very specific and has many faces. Its stepping pattern is so distinct that even those who do not study martial arts must notice it.

The Goals of Circle Walking

Now that I have actually got you circle walking I should explain exactly what you are trying to do. The easiest way to grasp why these requirements are so stringent is to understand something of the martial goals associated with circle walking.

The first goal is to keep the center of gravity situated between the feet. This is aided, in part, by the back-weighted stance you maintain while walking. This stance should rest your weight about seventy per cent on the rear leg. This is easier said than done, since the natural instinct is to shift the weight to the front leg. To actually walk without shifting the weight forward, even transitionally, is a learned skill.

Watch people walking and you will notice something interesting: the majority of people thrust their legs forward and then lean a bit into their forward legs. That means that most people are very slightly but definitely falling as they walk. In Bagua Zhang you walk upright. The idea is to be able to stop in mid-stride if necessary.

Scissors Steps

One way to keep the center of gravity under control is known as "scissors stepping." This is not too difficult; simply requiring that the inside of the legs brush against one another on every step. This happens in the transition: as the rear leg passes the front leg, you make sure they brush. When watching a Bagua expert walking the circle you should hear a swish-swish sound on each step. Even though the scissors steps and their sibilant sound simply signal that the legs brush one another, none of this means that the step has to be narrow. This is an important idea and you should review it; understanding this will render your Bagua walking much easier.

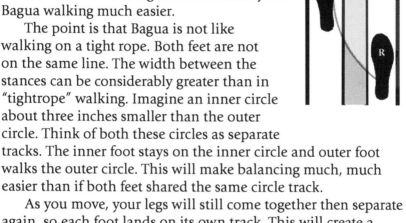

The point is that Bagua is not like walking on a tight rope. Both feet are not on the same line. The width between the stances can be considerably greater than in "tightrope" walking. Imagine an inner circle about three inches smaller than the outer circle. Think of both these circles as separate tracks. The inner foot stays on the inner circle and outer foot walks the outer circle. This will make balancing much, much easier than if both feet shared the same circle track.

As you move, your legs will still come together then separate again, so each foot lands on its own track. This will create a slight sense of swaying as you walk, but not much, certainly not enough to off-balance you. This is a method to break the notion that the feet have to step almost on top of one another. The proper walking method in Bagua Zhang is a combination of scissors legs and just the right width between the feet.

A Bagua Mistake

Since we are talking about the width of the feet and the tracing of the circle, let me take a moment and make the point that the feet should NEVER step in a true tightrope method, one foot directly in front of the other. In martial practice this is known as Closing the Door. It means, that the rear foot is blocked and has to step AROUND the front foot. This is definitely counter-indicated in just about every martial art, however it is very easy to make this mistake in Bagua Zhang walking. Be vigilant and do not allow closing to become a habit.

The Mud Treading Step

This is a good time to make the point that not all styles of Kung Fu start at the same level. Some styles start at high school or even college level. Some are perfect for preschoolers. Bagua is a college level style. It can be enjoyed by the non-expert just as some college courses can. But to really benefit thoroughly from the style, one should have at least a "higher education" attitude. Here's a good example of a simple/profound movement.

The mud step can be described in many ways. The name refers to the days when Beijing was mostly unpaved, crisscrossed with alleys which, during the rainy season, would become so muddy as to be almost non-navigable. Beijing residents came up with a unique solution. They wore shoes with long needles protruding from the soles which caught and secured traction much like cleats on soccer shoes. It must have looked eccentric at the time, but this characteristic method of walking required the hardy soul to lift the foot directly up so the needles would not drag and place it vertically downward to keep the ankle from turning. This idiosyncratic way of stepping was awkward but for the Bagua Zhang loving denizens of Beijing, it gave at least the impression of their own special stepping style. We are not entirely sure which form of stepping influenced the other. I like to take the position that there was some degree of reciprocity in the process.

Looking at the mud step from a structural and functional stand point will most quickly reveal the point of the pattern. Minor variations will not be a source of concern. In mud stepping the concept is the key concern; the form follows.

Mud Step: Described

In the Mud Step, try not to roll the heel up as you walk. This is a difficult requirement and even experts only accomplish it to varying degrees of imperfection. In essence the foot is held, through the entire stepping action, as though the sole were perfectly flat and parallel to the ground. Most people can accomplish this in regard to the placing of the foot in front of them. What they often overlook, just like the old adage "out of sight out of mind," is the portion of the step before reaching the other leg, when the rear leg scooches up from behind to kiss the front leg.

In that moment the heel escapes notice and naturally rolls before joining the front leg. In Bagua, we attempt to keep the sole of the moving foot parallel to the ground through the whole process of the step, as though it were floating on a very thin bed of air. We avoid sliding, though. The proper movement lifts the entire foot, moves it forward and then drops it as low to the ground as possible, but with a minimum of sliding contact.

Moving like this is sometimes called "flat walking".It doubles up with that other sophisticated component of Bagua Zhang walking: the control of weight. Bagua Zhang walking keeps the weight on the rear leg more while executing a flat step. It's a whole lot of coordination but, luckily, it is something that you can review every practice, making gradual progress through, forgive me, "baby steps" as you go round and round.

Weight and Walking:

This weight-back distribution is definitely not an intuitive method of movement. But by keeping weight back the Bagua expert moves without unduly throwing the chest or hips forward. Next time you are down at the mall, take a moment to increase your Bagua knowledge by doing some research. Watch everyone going about her business and you will notice that people have all sorts of leading edges. This is particularly evident when they turn in one direction or another. What this indicates is the tendency of most people to push forward a specific part of their body before turning in any direction. The range of leading edges is actually quite amazing. Some people lead from their jaws, others from their hearts turning those parts in the new direction a fraction of second before actually making the turn. But that's not all. You will see that some people actually lead with their eyes, their navels, their shoulders: all sorts of variations. The most common, especially among women, is leading with the front of the chest—in other words: the heart.

If you scrutinize a Bagua practitioner walking the circle it should be difficult if not impossible to catch a specific leading edge other than, possibly, the toes. In essence, the body moves as a completely integrated unit, somewhat statuesque but not statue-like. The weight is seated squarely above the feet allowing for very fast reversals of direction. It is such reversals, Threading and Palm Changes, which I will now bring to your attention.

The Basic Hand Position

To understand the next stage of training you will need a basic hand position as you walk the circle. This one, known as the Dragon, has you holding the fingers of each hand together, with  the fingertips of both hands pointing to the center of the circle. The inner hand will carry the fingertips about nose high. The outer hand will hold them just facing the inside of the inner elbow. If you are not performing an animal, this should be your default posture. As you walk clockwise (Yang direction) or counter-clockwise (Yin direction) keep the fingertips aimed at the circle center.

Turning Around and Changing Direction

Walking and turning: these are at the core of Bagua Zhang skills. I have already introduced you to the walking. Now you will take on the skill of reversing the direction of your walk. The first thing you should know is that it is a practiced skill and will require some study. As you will find out during continued experimentation and practice, if you have walked some ways in one direction, reversing and going the opposite way is like visiting an entirely new landscape.

Let's start from a martial standpoint and examine what "reversing direction" means, and why it must be so specific. Remember, even if you have very little interest in the martial application, it is the "story" which we are enacting, and following the martial is also the key to all the other benefits. Basically, you are doing one of the hardest things in the arts, namely, driving in one direction then flipping into the other direction. This potential for an extreme change of direction adds tremendous energy to the art. This is one reason, when you walk the circle, you should try to keep the majority of your weight back on the rear leg. Imagine you were rapidly walking in one direction and had to suddenly change. If your weight is loaded forward such a quick reversal is almost impossible, because you are essentially running nose first into the turn. That makes things decidedly more difficult.

Inside and Outside Reversals

There is a Yin and Yang to turning and it is pretty simple. If you begin a reversal with the outer leg forward you will find that you must turn to the inside of the circle, toward the center of the circle. If you make your transition in this manner it is called an INSIDE Palm Change. If you begin turning with the inner leg foremost, you will have to turn your back on the center of the circle and thereby execute what we call an OUTSIDE Palm Change. Every single animal can reverse direction through either an INSIDE or OUTSIDE change. In simplest terms the OUTSIDE change takes your eyes off the center of the circle. During the INSIDE change you keep looking right at the circle center.

Now let's describe the INSIDE turn, simplest of all direction changes. If you learn this one you can basically change from any position to any other in the Bagua world. I will start the description with you walking around a circle, counter-clockwise.

Threading a Palm Change

Start by walking the circle with the basic hand position, left hand pointed toward the center. When you stop walking, you are facing the Yin (counter-clockwise) direction with the right foot forward. As you perform the reversal to the opposite direction have the two hands exchange positions just like they are pulley-connected. Make the left hand retract to the guard position as the right hand extends toward the centerpoint. This hand movement, called Threading, is relatively easy. You want to time it so it pretty much synchronizes with the closing and opening of your feet. Start the hands and legs together and end the hands and legs together. This entire process of turning the feet and switching the hands along with reversing direction is known as a Basic Palm Change.

I will go over it again because it is so important:

You stop with the outside (right) foot forward. If you are walking counter-clockwise you cannot do the INSIDE change any other way.

Turn to the left, but very slowly. Your left hand draws in while your right hand extends parallel to your left retracting forearm and toward the

12   *Bagua Zhang's Animals*

center of the circle.

By the time you have turned to the clockwise direction, your right hand has taken its place as the lead hand. Your right toe has turned inward, pivoting on your right heel.

Then your left heel pivots outward and Voila! You have completed a change, and you are facing the opposite direction on the circle.

KEYS:
Note the following fascinating points and neurological tidbits:

1. Bagua is a cross-lateral art. That means the nerves on one side of the body interact with those on the other side. As you turn from a Yin to a Yang circle, for instance, your right toe turns inward and you begin to withdraw your left hand. As your left foot rotates outward, you thread toward the center of the circle with the right hand. That's right, the hands and legs are related to each other across the body in what you might think of as a diagonal scheme.

2. Don't fret. If you can't do it just this way or have to do it in smaller parts, that just means you are a normal human being. Practice will help and, in the case of Bagua in particular, we take refuge in the quotation from the Dao De Jing of Lao Tzu, "Nature is self correcting."

You have successfully completed one circle shift and are now walking in the opposite direction. Don't even try it from the opposite side. Just go back and try the counter-clockwise change many more ten times before even trying the clockwise change. This is the best way to approach learning this skill. But just to show you that I have been teaching for decades and KNOW you will want to try the opposite action I will avert my eyes and go out for a quiet cup of Kuan Yin tea...

3.... OK, I'm back. You may walk the circle slowly at first, or not. But I strongly advise you to perform the changes slowly. Not only are they a bit complicated technically, but you want to take the time to actually FEEL what's going on during each change. A slow, controlled execution aids in that more than you could guess. This is just about the most basic change you can make.

Circling Basics

Why are changes so important? Well, to start with, Bagua is an art of angles and circles (really, every martial art is, but Bagua is obsessed.) To successfully use an angle in a fight you have to be able to alter that angle and even, in extreme cases, reverse it—and fast. Direction change, though probably not used that often at the extreme of 180°, is essential to the practice of the art. Preparing for direction change by keeping the correct structure with the spine erect and the weight back also has the benefit of augmenting the health and postural benefits of the practice. So, if you have problems executing the change, first look to your posture. You are probably leaning forward just before you make the change.

The Outside Palm Change

If the INSIDE THREAD is the easiest change, the OUTSIDE THREAD is pretty close. In this case you are walking in the counter clockwise direction, and this time you halt with the inner, left leg forward. The actions you are about to perform will be basically the same. But since you are turning away from the circle center with your back to it, they may feel different. Nonetheless, here goes. Turn your left toe inward, pivoting on the heel as always. Your left hand tracks horizontally to the right and away from the center of the circle. Continue the turning action and let the right foot pivot rightward until it is aligned on the circumference. The arms continue past that point, turning rightward until the right hand is the lead and pointed to the circle. They

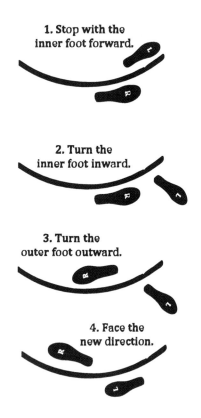

1. Stop with the inner foot forward.

2. Turn the inner foot inward.

3. Turn the outer foot outward.

4. Face the new direction.

14   *Bagua Zhang's Animals*

still thread one another but your turning will make them appear to cut big swathes in the air, like twin sabers. In other words turn AWAY from the circle instead of into it. It's that simple. Though it seems a little wild and wooly it is, in actuality, a little easier and even feels a little more natural. Why? Remember what I said about the INSIDE change? That it was a little cross-wired according to arms and legs. Well, the OUTSIDE change is not. First the entire left hemisphere moves: arm, legs, toes, everything. Then the right hemisphere opens up. There is little cross body action here. Since the hands get to whirl and spin, and the body turning and weight shifting are a little more open and free, many people find that they can actually perform the OUTSIDE change easier and faster than the INSIDE version.

Gentlemen, Start Your Circles

Let's review. You now know how to walk a circle. You do so with the right stepping pattern, the correct weight distribution, and the appropriate speed. You can stop at any moment, with either foot forward. Then you are able to execute a change of direction known as a Palm Change. Once that has been completed, you walk in the other direction and choose your own options.

In other words you have the basic actions of this fabulous art and are ready to learn the Eight Animals of Bagua Zhang.

The Inside Palm Change Foot Pattern

1. Walk the circle CCW. Stop when the outer (right) foot is in the lead position.

2. Turn the toe of the outer foot inward and past the circle centerpoint.

When you change directions by turning INTO the circle this is called an Inside Change. No matter the animal, the stepping pattern will be essentially the same.

3. Next turn the inner (left) toe to the left and move that foot a little to the side and outside the circle.

4. Once you have made the turn, go ahead and begin walking the circle in the new CW, Yang, direction.

The Outside Palm Change Foot Pattern

1. Walk the circle CCW. Stop when the inner (left) foot is in the lead position.

2. Turn the toe of the inner foot inward and to the right. Your back is now turned away from the center of the circle.

When you change directions by turning AWAY from the circle, this is called an Outside Change. Regardless of the animal, the Outside stepping pattern will be essentially the same.

3. Next turn the right toe to the left and move that foot a little to the side and inside the circle.

4. Once you have made the turn, go ahead and begin walking the circle in the new CW, Yang, direction.

Tip to Toe Walking Tips

Here is a list of key points as you walk the circle. Do not, I repeat, do not trouble yourself to insanity by trying to apply all the ideas at the same moment. We are touring from the tips of the toes to the top of the head. Pick an area to refine each practice session and progress will come fairly easily.

1. **Toes point in the direction of the circle.** This is one of the hardest to check unless you want to spend all your practice time with your head hanging down. The culprit will probably be the inner foot. The inner toe advances as it should but just at the end of the move the heel spins forward and plants itself in the path of the outer foot. Solution: Imagine the toes dragging the rest of the foot along the circumference.

2. **Heels Do Not Lift.** Each Bagua step barely raises the back heel off the ground. If done really well the gap between the heel and the floor is invisible. This requires a tensing of the ankle and a controlled shifting of the weight at the right time.

3. **Knees Support Each Other.** Bagua steps start small and consistent. One foot does not get too far from the other. It feels as though there were a big rubber band holding yours knees close to one another. Supporting one another means that both knees and feet relate to one another every moment.

4. **Buttocks Sit.** Imagine that you are perching on the edge of a bench or chair. You sink just enough to feel engagement in your lower back. Sitting down consolidates your entire body. Just sit a little and, try not to stand up.

5. **Ribcage Lifts.** Gently try to lift your rib cage. This is accomplished by imagining the ribcage floating upward, extending the middle back. There will be some stomach tensing but just enough to perform the right actions.

6. **Spine Rotates.** As you face the circle center you should twist the spine at least a little. You will feel some of this in the waist especially as you turn inward on those animals which have an extra torque such as the Eagle.

7. **Chin Retreats.** Pull in the chin as though you were pushing it toward the back of your neck. Imagine someone pushing directly back on the front of your jaw. This will lengthen the cervical vertebrae.

8. **Shoulders Droop.** Your shoulders should feel as though

each one has a ten pound sand bag pulling down on them. If done right this can be relaxing when you achieve the feeling that weights are actually slipping off your shoulders.

    9. Elbows Hang. You should imagine heavy weight attached to your elbows, pulling them downward.

    10. Neck Turns. One of Bagua's benefits comes from the constant turning of the neck. This has all sorts of neurological effects, helping to keep your entire upper body mobile and healthy.

    11. Eyes Lead. The eyes and the neck are intimately linked. Many nerve pathways in the neck are controlled by eye movement. Especially when you turn, the eyes should "lead" the movement gazing slightly ahead and beyond your actions.

    12. Crown Floats. The top of the head should be as light as a bobbing balloon. Though most of the actions in Bagua have a slight sinking feeling to them, the neck and head remain upright and light, otherwise your movements will not be agile and responsive.

    As you can tell, the practice of Bagua is not just physical. On the other hand the details of walking are listed here to forget for now and remember only when experienced. As you study Bagua, as it deepens and becomes richer, you will realize that these are not so much rules and regulations as little discoveries. When you first grasp the relation of the neck and the eyes it will be a revelation affecting every aspects of your practice. Walk and learn, and everything will take care of itself.

General Comments on the Animals

Because they are so fundamental, there is a tendency among some Bagua practitioners to de-emphasize the animals palms. They don't seem as interesting or dynamic as other aspects of the art. Since there is less movement in them they certainly are not as exotic as the famous Eight Changing Palms which most people associate with Bagua.

It's very similar to the situation in Tai Chi practice. Long time players know that the real TC practice often encompasses Qigong, standing practice, energy issuance, weapons training, push hands and applications. In fact, it is entirely possible to not only get a good TC workout without doing the ubiquitous TC solo set, but even to advance to a higher level without the set or, at least, having abandoned the set after a certain point in the training; as we are told, the practitioner Cheng Man-Ching rarely practiced the entire set after a specific point in his training. Even further, we might say that it is almost impossible to master the art of TC just by sticking to the set.

Think of the Bagua animals as the basic numbers in arithmetic. Even higher math is dependent on these. And the famous Changing Palms are just examples of the recombination of these and some additional basic elements. But the real differentiation starts in the Yin and Yang Palm Changes and the Eight Animals.

And what do the animals contain that's so important to most Bagua practice? Let's examine them from a strictly functional standpoint, without external considerations such as philosophical or medical beliefs. This might be a good place to think about these weird positions in short, plain descriptive language.

LION: Palms facing one another. Fingertips pushed toward the circle like twin spear hands. Compressing the hands on a vertical line. The inner hand lifting.

SNAKE: Pushing down and forward like rolling a log to the front. The back hand ready to follow the front hand as it thrusts forward.

BEAR: Rotating the forearms inward. Some downward pressing from the palms.

PHOENIX/DRAGON: Rotating the palms outward. Trying to keep the arms on line with one another.

EAGLE: Pushing the edge of one arm inward while pushing the outside edge outward. Lifting energy but focusing on the ulnar side of the major hand and the radial side of the minor one.

HAWK: If the Eagle expands, the Hawk contracts. Spiral energy on the ulna edge but due to a different pivot point (shoulder, not waist) an inward rotation toward the medial line.

UNICORN: Like Snake in the opposite direction. Like Phoenix with its emphasis on the back of the hand. Contracting, hooking inward action.

APE: Vertical contracting rotation. One hand inward the other outward. Both hand emphasize major rotation along the forearm axis.

The Shapes of the Animal Palms

How you hold your palms in Bagua Zhang is very specific to each animal. And I will go into that in a minute. But, before I do, you have a chance here to look at the general significance of the palm in this art.

First, what could not be said too often: The Palm is the Body. This is a concept that the aspiring Bagua expert must understand: that each palm represents an entire hemisphere of the body. The right palm, from a Bagua standpoint, stretches directly through the torso down to the right foot. What this means is that we don't think of the limbs as stuck into the body but intimately connected with the body and, conversely, requiring the entire side of the body to actively motivate even the smallest action of the palm.

Imagine moving your right palm. Better yet, do that action. Now imagine yourself encased in a flexible body suit constructed in such a way that you cannot budge your right palm without moving that entire side of your body.

Animal Characteristics

As in Chinese astrology, each animal has a distinct and complex personality. You can play into these traits such as attempting to be inspired by the actions of a gliding eagle or slippery snake.

Take a lion. He starts off in so many Bagua styles and there must be a reason. He is noble and we associate nobility with a way of holding oneself which we often call manner, or, most perfectly for our example, CARRIAGE. Compared to the Tiger energy of so many Kung Fu styles, the Lion is just as fierce but more direct, and stronger. He is the straight line of Bagua. Since Bagua is an elusive, subtle and somewhat complex style, we begin with a good solid structure with which to walk the circle, <u>and</u> a direct, straight line. It's almost like a farewell to the world we are leaving, a last glance at the relatively simple world of the martial equivalent of Euclidean geometry. From Lion on, the curve rules.

But there is another layer here. The Chinese Lion is also a playful creature. During ritual dancing, the Lion is shown with an assistant and a ball. The two-man Lion and the assistant then play acrobatic tricks, all based on the feline nature loving a ball. Bagua even has a move imitating this cat-like ball action in the very first posture we see of the Lion.

You've met people like this: seemingly controlled and austere on the outside with a hidden playful, nature that can delight but also confuse you. Though the Lion is authentically playful it is the hidden aspect of this quality that keeps you guessing, and even adds danger to the mix. That's not to mention that the obvious or Ming ("bright," as opposed to An, or dark and hidden) nature of the Lion is actually a balance of Yin and Yang all by itself. The stereotypical Lion is noble, yes, but he is also fierce and this fierceness can boil up like temper. When the Lion is at play this is even more dodgey, because the play can turn terrible in an instant. In martial arts the Lion is the direct fighter who, once he decides to come, is almost unstoppable. The confusing signal, always a necessary component, is the playful nature that makes WHEN he is coming into a deadly guessing game.

Each animal is represented with distinct characteristics. As you practice them, these traits will show themselves in the interpretation of your movements.

On Practicing the Animals

Each of the eight trigrams represents a direction on the compass such as south, east or northwest. Each of these eight divisions is sometimes called a "palace." And, in addition, there is always a ninth palace in the world of Bagua Zhang. The ninth palace is where you stand with the other eight surrounding you. It is located in the center of the other eight and becomes, by its very centrality, a sort of celestial pivot point. I hold the compass in my hand and stand on the mesa where the stars stare at me from the eight directions. I squint to read the compass face, yes, eight directions but after all that is judging from my position in the universe at this moment and from that the directions are given their frame.

In Bagua Zhang we practice the Eight Animal moves as a fundamental method. But of course there is a ninth animal: Man. It is Man's ability to initiate, to borrow, to subsume, alter and adapt that makes each experience of the animal practice just that much more poignant. When the Lion acts like a lion, his choice is non-existent. Unless he is mad or drugged, when a man acts like a lion he chooses to do so and therefore never completely loses his humanity. He puts on the skin but does not trade the bones as it were. And yet it is consciousness itself which we must shift to "play" the Bagua Zhang animals.

Let's be honest. Each of us has encountered people who we could not convince ourselves were not some animal passing itself off for a person. I don't mean just the boorish and loud, crude imitators of animals, who can capture none of the animal's native dignity. I mean that fellow in your office who doesn't actually resemble a snake so much as make you think of one. Gallant lions and playful monkeys abound in human life. In a sense, their imitation is just the martial equivalent of changing masks: spies, too, are martial artists who use misdirection as their skill.

But let's go deeper. When we see the cat move, we are impressed by its agility and grace. But if we drop the cliches and really look, we are drawn into less obvious perceptions. Even the most talented or graceful human rarely moves like an animal in its completeness. The panther twitches a muscle and the action ripples the shine all the way through its pelt. The snake motivates itself from some hidden motor which animates its entire being all at once and continually. The monkey preens itself calmly, but even in the most lackadaisical moment is riddled through with potential changeability and sudden agility.

It is this totality of the animal nature which makes it essential to practice in this manner. Martial arts taps areas of the brain almost abandoned by modern life: areas that access information so rapidly we can't even recognize the discernment while it is occurring. It's not enough to perform the animal motions. You must inhabit the animal while you walk. As you read about all these animal actions you will feel swamped by the technicalities at first. But as they fall into place, as you gain confidence and master form you will feel the animal natures emerge.

It should be obvious that the structure of the movements is a ladder to reach that anima-inspired state. And yet the feeling should never completely submerge the structure, the discipline and the control of the movement. It is the interplay of the two where things become really interesting. In Chinese philosophy this is known as Yong and Ti, use and structure, much as we might say Form and Function, but something a little deeper.

I make this point for a number of reasons, but one of the most important concerns what might be called "organic" martial arts. There is a widely held misconception that traditional martial arts are streamlined, beautiful, highly extended and dramatically constructed. Thousands of children throughout the world learn each year to pose in movements far more related to Beijing Opera than to any real martial heritage. It is no wonder that people are leaving traditional forms in droves after almost a half century of being improperly taught, and actually instructed in methods that never, I repeat never, existed in the real martial universe.

The animal methods are a perfect means of reinvigorating the organic shape of the practitioner. Contrary to the sanitized and misleading gymnastics often passed off as Bagua Zhang, the practitioner should keep his shape round, relaxed, alert and absolutely configured to his own personal posture.

Think of each animal in its completeness, not only as a posture. Each of the animals in Bagua Chang also has a series of changes. You will learn at least one change for each and when you perform it you must also keep the spirit of the animal intact. In other words, the Lion changes like a Lion, never dropping its manner.

Initially, the ORDER of the Animals is meant to help you

with memorizing and perfecting their characteristics. Obviously, they can be rearranged upon reaching some degree of confidence but I suggest that you keep to the order when first learning them. Though many people think of the core of Bagua Zhang living in the Eight Changing Palms, admittedly more sophisticated, this is not exactly the case. The animals are so well constructed that, in theory, they can bring a would-be expert all the way through Bagua Zhang training to its complete integration. They also have the important function of acting as Qigong exercises which, simultaneously, inhabit the Bagua Zhang world of constant movement. I will explore this later but now, as you are beginning the training of the animals, it is important to realize that they move through almost the entire spectrum of the art. It is my contention, and in fact the inspiration for this book, that the animals can lead not only to an understanding of the art but, due to their highly concentrated nature, also supply a valuable set of tools for mastery of true Bagua Zhang.

In many branches of BaGua Zhang the Lion is often the "standard" for the eight internal animals. The actions of the Lion are large and clean. One hand is held palm up, pointed toward the center of the circle. The other hand is held palm down, higher than the rear eyebrow. The top hand should not be directly over the bottom hand but appropriately off-angled. Your two hands are connected as though you were a lion holding an invisible ball between your paws. Sometimes the two hands are thought of as being the upper and lower JAWS of a lion. Stepping should be clean, upright and unhurried. The spine should be straight. The area of concentration is the neck including the upper back. This is one of the best circling exercises to begin a training session.

The Lion

Start the Lion practice by just walking around the circle. Do not even lift your hands. Just begin by walking at a quiet, unhurried pace. Shake your arms a bit to relax. Move continuously without worrying what you will be doing next. Eventually you will want to move your arms so bring them up into any position you choose. Keep your gaze high, seeking across the circle as though you were scanning a horizon in Africa. Lift your head and keep it straight. Your chin should push backward about a half inch as though someone were  placing a finger on the front of your chin and slightly, gently pushing. This will lengthen the vertebrae of your neck and virtually make you stand taller. This action (Yu Shen) is essential for Bagua and is wonderfully and importantly emphasized in the action of the Lion. When you feel your neck is straight, your gaze will be unhurried and steady, far-sighting and calm. You are ready.

Each of the Bagua animals has a basketful of fruits and nuts: surprising morsels of culture, practice, function, medicine, art and just plain fancy. I will concern myself with as many of these as I am able but, for now, I start with the technical and postural requirements. As they say in the practice of Qigong, first comes structure. And in the case of the Bagua animals structure is particularly important because it is what you hold onto while practicing an art that changes every moment.

Raise the inner hand (always the one closest to the center of the circle) with the palm up. We will assume that you are following the traditional procedure and begin the practice walking the circle in a counter-clockwise direction. All the instruction in this book will take this as your starting direction and make references conform to that idea. You are of course responsible for "flipping" the instructions at some point. Our suggestion is to get one side worked into your blood a bit before changing. If one side is solid and you know what you are doing it is like having an extra teacher helping you.

Your hand is raised in what we call the Yang position. This word has absolutely no connection to Yin and Yang. Rather it is another Chinese word connoting the action of raising something.

As you lift the Yang hand to about the height of your solar plexus you may find it a bit difficult to hold the arm in this position. This will be especially true if you find yourself stuffing your left elbow into the sides of your ribs. This puts stress on the shoulder and eventually fatigues the arm. Bagua is a relaxed art where you do work hard but you don't allow yourself to continue practicing movements which are actually incorrect and strain your body. Keep circling this way for a while; experiment by holding the Yang hand out at any height between your navel and your heart. Keep the palm facing upward.

Now, raise the rear hand (the one on the outside of the circle). Lift that hand with the palm facing downward. Your left (inner) hand points to the center of the circle with your left fingertips. Hold your outer right hand about a foot away from your right eyebrow at about the angle of 1:00 on a huge upright clock face. Another way to think about this is to imagine that you are the Lion Playing with the Ball—a famous movement in the Chinese Lion Dance. You might think you would want your right hand to float exactly above your left hand as though you were holding a huge ball. However you head is in the way so you hold that superior right hand a little off to one side, hence the angle of about 20° off center.

Despite this, the hands should feel as though they were connected, as though an invisible globe were being embraced by both of them at the same time. Not only this, but the wrists should follow the gentle curvature of the forearm in such a way that you have the feeling and look of holding the imaginary ball with the entirety of both arms, not just the hands.

The Lion Inside Change
This hand position provides the earliest and easiest change to accomplish when you move the Lion energy. Remember, when I say "changes" I refer to a series of actions that reverse your direction and send you walking in the opposite way.

Halt your walking with the right foot in the lead, and the hands in the Lion position. Bring the top hand down toward the bottom one. When they are about six inches apart revolve your hands clockwise as though you were really rotating a small ball held between your palms. At the same times turn the rights foot inward. Now start to separate the hands, with the left on top. Turn your left toes outward. Shift the majority of your weight to your right leg as you turn leftward. You have completed the change, exchanged both hands and now face in the opposite direction. Start walking this way and keep practicing the Lion.

As you work with this try to synchronize the leg change and the palm change. They don't have to move at the same rate but they should all end at the same moment.

The Lion Inside Change

1. Stop walking CCW and freeze with the right foot forward.

2. Bring the right upper hand down to the left palm as though slapping...

3. Rotate the two hands CW as though rolling a small ball.

4. Turn both feet leftward and separate your hands to reverse the Lion posture.

The Lion 35

The Lion Inside Change: Details

1. As you walk in the Yin (CCW) direction you hold the right hand up and the left centered...

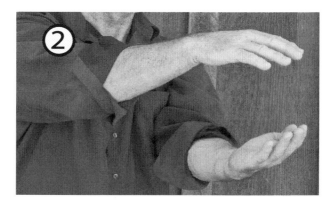

2. Bring the top hand down to the bottom almost as though you were slapping them together.

3. Not only do you **not** have to slap your hands together, you will find it easier if the hands do not touch. Roll the hands CW as though holding a small ball.

4. Revolve the hands until they have reversed; the left is now on top.

5. Then pull the left up until you are in the Lion posture, walking in the new direction.

The Outside Change

When you turn AWAY from the center you are performing an Outside Change. At some point your back will be turned to the centerpoint of the circle. Outside Changes take a little more time to complete than the Inside Changes since you are going "the long way" round. The hand actions are essentially the same.

1. Walking in the Yin direction (CCW) stop when the left (inside) foot is in the lead position.

2. Turn to your right while bringing both hands together. At the same time turn the left foot toward your center.

3. As you turn, roll the hands CW around each other until they have reversed position.

4. Continue turning right. Begin to separate the hands into the Lion Plays with Ball posture. At the same time, turn the right toes outward.

5. Stop turning when you have reversed the position and are now walking CW around the circle.

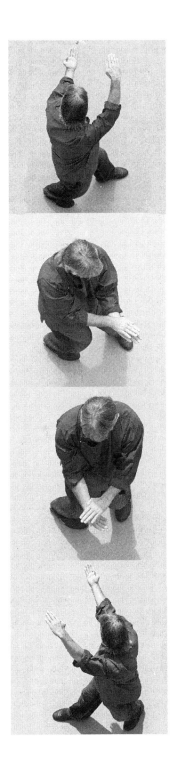

The Lion
Orientation: All fingertips point to center
Lead: Fingertips and back of hand
Associated Trigram: Qian, The Creative
Represents Heaven
Body: The neck and head
Medical: Pericardium Channel

Clapping Hands

Here is a method one of my teachers, Adam Hsu, employed to show us the correct feeling of the Lion. It works great at unifying the two hands if you do it right. As you walk the circle, bring the high hand down onto the lower hand with a slapping action as though you were catching a fly between your palms. You need not clap so hard you hurt yourself but be definite. Once your hands are down slowly raise the upper hand in the Ball-carrying position. The feeling of the connection between yours palms, a little ghostly once you've separated your hands, should stay with you as you stretch out your arms. Do this as much as you need while circling. The slapping cross wires your kinesthetic perception and gives you that valuable sense of connection between the hands.

Bagua Eyes

Also, you always training your eyes when practicing Bagua. Make sure your right, high hand is inside the range of your peripheral vision as you walk, just kissing what would be the right upper corner of this field of vision. Now you have the basic Lion posture. Take a moment to check yourself on the following points:

    1. Keep your head straight up with the cervical vertebrae suspended.

    2. Try to feel a circular and continuous connection going right through your shoulders and connecting both arms as though they shared a single pulley.

    3. Point both sets of fingers toward the center of the circle and, as you walk, keep concentrating on stretching them toward the center as though projecting a beam of light across the circle.

For thousands of years the Chinese have respected the Snake. They see it as intimately tied to the Dragon. Wise and intuitive, the Snake controls others through intelligence and guile. Snake movements are not only a perfect example of its slithering approach, but also resembles the ancient symbol of water and its respective trigram. Snake style Kung Fu utilizes numerous portions of the arms, which they see as the Snake's head, body, tail and fangs. Each movement wraps some limb as though it were the body of a serpent. Additionally, strikes are aimed at vital points and nerve centers, replicating the snake's paralytic venom. If the movements of the Lion represent straight and true actions, the Snake is the essence of indirect. Where the Lion holds up its head, the Snake presses its belly against the earth and moves like its trigram equivalent: flowing water. The realm of the Snake corresponds to the kidneys. Think of a snake's body wriggling along the ground, the locomotion originating in the integrated action of the entire snake body. Control of the kidneys is the key to creating movements which "shimmy" through the entire length of the body. The snake moves from side to side, slowly and patiently lulling the enemy into a stupor of expectancy—then it strikes.

The Snake

The movements of the Snake are unhurried and continuous. The Snake moves in a determined and controlled order. He undulates and wriggles, but his progress can be amazingly swift. It is the sort of movement that you can never forget if you hold his body and sense the cascade of his slithering energy.

Start the Snake movement by placing the inside hand at the height of the waist, palm down, fingers pointing toward the circle center. The forearm is basically level to the ground, with the elbow in proximity of the rib cage. The outside hand pretty much mirrors the inside hand, with that palm also turned downward. Since the inner hand is almost directly pointed to the center, the outside hand is slightly offset; they cannot both occupy the same place. I tell students that it is as if one snake were entering a tube and the other is right behind it, off to an angle, waiting for its turn. Think of the rear hand contouring around your belly. While one hand is obviously the dominant one, the other is quite strongly engaged. That rear hand, trying to move toward the center of the circle causes a definite outward waist turn at the height of the hands.

This makes a perfect complement to the idea of the Snake concentrating on the kidneys. As you walk the circle you send energy to the kidneys, somewhat like tightening your stomach muscles, though not so rigidly. The kidney extended in this manner should feel like a bicycle tire circling the middle.

The Inside Snake Change

1. Since you will start the circle walk in the CCW direction this designates your left hand as the inside limb. Walk the circle with the Snake posture for a while. Finally, you decide to practice the basic Snake Change. Stop with the outside, right, foot forward.

2. Turn the right toe inward into a kou bu. Try to rotate enough to touch your knees together. Retract the left hand toward the midline of your body. At about this time you will be facing the center of the circle.

3. Begin to open the left foot with the majority of the weight shifting to the right foot. At the same time, extend the right hand, palm down, by sliding your right forearm directly over your left (without touching each other.) Your right fingertips should point to the circle center through the whole process.

4. You will now have reversed the posture with the right inner foot and the left outer foot pointing along the circle CW. Now begin walking in the new direction.

The Snake   45

The Snake
Orientation: Front fingertips point to center, rear fingers point to front wrist.
Lead: Fingertips and palms.
Associated Trigram: Kan, The Abysmal
Represents Water
Body: The kidneys
Medical: Kidney Channel

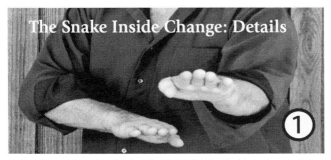

The Snake Inside Change: Details

1. Walking the Circle in the Yin (CCW) direction with the left hand extended...

2. Slide the right hand over the right from above, like a snake slithering past another...

3. At the same time retract the left hand.

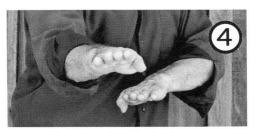

4. Now, right hand in the lead, you are now back to walking in the Yang (CW) direction.

The Snake Outside Change:
Once again you are walking the circle CCW with the left hand on the inside. Stop when the left inner foot is forward. Turn the left toe inward in a kou bu step. Turn toward the right while retracting the left hand. The continued rotation of your body to the right should turn the right toe outward until it is parallel to the perimeter of the circle. At the same time, the right fingertips extend toward the centerpoint. Once you have made the change continue walking the circle
in the new direction.

Keys:
The transformation of the Snake from one direction to the other is just another example of the Threading action so common in Bagua. You can, of course, pass the hands in many variations, but the most common and classical one to start with is that of the new dominant hand passing directly on top of the retracting one. Once you've made the change, bring your energy to the very tips of your fingers. Keep them scrupulously pointed to the center of the circle. The Snake energy is a combination of gentle but persistent downward and forward pushing, like a serpent slithering through the grass.

Outside Change:
1. Stop with the left (inner) foot in the lead... (You are seeing these photos from outside the circle.)

2. Rotate your left toe in (kou bu). Turn to the right, keeping your hands relatively fixed in place...

3. Slide the right hand over the left as you turn to the right, back to the center. Start turning your right toe out (bai bu)....

4. Stop turning when you are back on the circle, now with the right hand pointing to center.

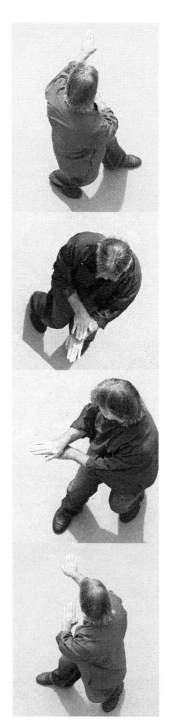

The Snake

The Half-Circle Breath: Lion and Snake

Here is a great Qigong method to practice with any of the animals. It will not only relax you, but it will help to clarify key points on each animal.

Mentally divide the circle in half. Now walk the circle in the Snake position, half way round while inhaling. As you inhale, keep to the general shape of the Snake but completely relax. You should feel the position get a little "soft" because you are relaxing your muscles. When you reach the half-way point begin to exhale. As you do this you put some force into the Snake. You do not change the position but, like dynamic tension, you press down harder with both hands while trying to stretch them forward as though sliding them along a desktop. The strengthening of the position is barely visible. It is like you are pushing a huge weight you cannot move. As you attempt this, try to imagine someone about to strike you in the kidneys and try to protect yourself by strengthening your lower back area. This is said to increase the body's Wei Qi or "protective energy." The kidneys are connected to the element of Water, the Snake's trigram. When you reach the beginning, having completed one entire circle, you once again begin the inhalation and relax your posture. Do this many times. This will tremendously help your body to accept the Snake posture, and to understand where the intent of the movement lies.

Now try the same exercise with the Lion. As you walk inhale and relax. When you exhale squeeze the invisible ball that the Lion holds between your palms. Stiffen the fingers with the intent of pushing them forward. Concentrate the tightening on your neck muscles. The Lion represents the clarity and directness of the Heaven trigram. As you walk, you will feel which muscles to tense and which are just for support. This exercise can work with any of the animals and, since you now know two of them, try this...

Walk one round with the Lion and the next with the Snake. Change the breathing and the tensing appropriately. If you prefer you can, of course, do three rounds or any number of each animal. The idea is to get a clear contrast between the two animals in posture and intent.

This will work for any sequence of animals but the Lion and the Snake have a particular relationship. You will learn that each posture in the series encourages some change in your torso.

Indeed, all changes in the animal series are centered on the torso. No animal pattern solely concentrates on the legs, or the arms. It is the torso that requires the most training in authentic Chinese martial arts. Starting with the Lion, concentrate on the neck. Then, as you switch to the Snake, lower your attention to the kidneys. This extreme change of intent shows that these first two animals range all the way from the top of the torso to the bottom. The experience of practicing this foreshadows all the other animal changes, and ranges the spectrum of the exercises. Just practicing the Lion and the Snake will give you a sharp sense of the relation between intent and feeling, a key aspect of the animal training.

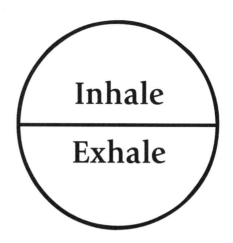

The benefits of walking the Bear include relaxing and opening the shoulders. The position of the hands and the rotation of the arms aid this effect. The power of the Bear derives in some part from his relaxed heaviness. Standing man-like, the bear rears and slaps. The energy of the Bear opens the back, and thereby aids the spine, the vital area for Bagua excellence. The Bear encourages dropping your center of gravity and firmly connecting with the earth. Its trigram is the mountain, a good representation of the Bear's essence.

The Bear

Over fifteen hundred years ago, one of China's greatest doctors, Hua Tuo, developed a series of exercises based on five archetypal forms of movement. These Five Animals greatly influenced Chinese medical practice, especially in regard to physical fitness and longevity. One of the key animals in this exercise was the Bear, known for its loose, heavy and powerful movements. The Bear, though not a common or well-known style of Kung Fu, is nonetheless a formidable type of movement reflected in many great Kung Fu styles such as Baji and Bagua. In classical Chinese medical  practice Bearish style postures and movements are said to relax the body, loosen the muscles and add thickness to the bones. The organ associated with the Bear is the kidneys, same as the Snake, but with a different, heavier, feeling. Bear motions often lower the body, relax the muscles and attempt to "sink" the center of gravity. The energy of the Bear focuses on the back of the body. As you perform the Bear, you should relax completely.

    Start the Bear by dropping the hands palms downward. It is best to begin with the fingers pointing forward. The arms should be held bent into a bow shape. The shoulders should be drooped and the back expanded. In other words, think of pressing both palms down on a table top. Roll the elbows outward so the little finger edges of the forearms face forward, the fingertips of each hand now point to one another. The shoulders now roll forward just a bit more. The entire structure should feel as though you are blocking with your forearm, an inverted block which is similar to Wing Chun Pai's Wing Block, or the Tangle from Tai Chi Chuan. The back, especially the upper back, should be as relaxed as possible. It should also feel as though it were spreading outward. Picture your back as melting wax, spreading down and outward. As you walk the

The Bear

circle, slightly turn the waist so that the inner elbow basically points past the center while the outer elbow rides a little ahead. In other words the two elbows do not exactly align with one another. The rear hand should be offset enough to be able to "see" the center of the circle. Turn your face directly toward the center with enough rotation in the neck to aid in the turning of waist. The Bear keeps this structure all the way through the walking exercise, circle after circle. But if you do this with stiffness or a frozen posture, and attitude you are violating the very concept of the Bear. This animal is firm, powerful, and yet, loose as can be. Think of lumbering without actually swaying from side to side. If you think you are heavy, it's time to get heavier. Let your feet sink into the earth the way water vanishes into parched ground. Water has the energy of flowing downward, and so does the Bear. There is, literally, no point at which the Bear stands up. Sometimes in practice we imagine we are descending a flight of stairs. How does the Bear continually sink without taking a break, then raising up so you can go down again? It is simple to say, but will take a little practice. The secret lies in what some people call rebound energy. As you shift your weight onto the left leg the right leg, on release, naturally straightens a bit like a spring expanding so, when you shift weight back to the right, it has spontaneously reset to receive the dropping weight of the Bear Step.

Dr. Hua Tuo's version of the Bear

More about Bear energy

Strangely, there happens to be <u>eight</u> types of bears. Bagua's Bear is most probably the Asiatic Black (Ursus Thibetanus). Indeed, references to him in the art always mention the Hei Xiong or Black Bear. This species, which resembles his American relative, spends his time foraging in trees. His beautiful  black fur is contrasted to a white splashy breast patch, giving him a natural Yin/Yang resonance as though he were the walking, growling "dark fish, white eye" side of the symbol. The Black Bear stands over six feet tall, weighs in excess of 400 pounds, and humans who stumble upon him are not always lucky enough to escape whole. On the other hand men hunt the Black Bear for use in medical formulae while also pushing him back further and further into the forests beyond ever encroaching farm lands. The Black Bear stands upright but sways somewhat while he surveys the landscape.

 In Bagua you imitate the two drooping arms representing the front paws which, though suspended, should feel that they might at any moment drop back to earth. This sensation captures the bear's feeling of heavy, loose energy. We are reminded of the story of Yang Chen Fu, the great master of the Yang style Tai Chi, walking with a disciple through the streets. A teamster cart breaks loose and starts rolling down the street, unattended. It rolls right toward Yang Sifu who bounces it off to the side of the road without halting the conversation he is having with his student. The "kao jin" or leaning energy of Tai Chi has this Bear-like quality. Bagua has it too. Practice slowly, shifting your weight from side to side. But keep your shoulders inside the limits of your feet. It is too easy, when practicing to lean too far in the direction of your power.

The Bear Inside Change

Turning is a specialty of the Bear, whether he is scratching his back on a tree or turning to regard you and your supply of camping food. The movement called Black Bear Turns Back is common to almost every style of Bagua Zhang.

The direction change in the middle of circle walking models itself after this mammoth animal but is essentially a graceful action.

1. You are walking the circle counter-clockwise. Halt with the right outside foot in the lead.

2. Rotate both arms outward as you turn in (kou bu) the right foot.

56 *Bagua Zhang's Animals*

3. Continue the waist rotation to the left while turning out the left foot (bai bu). Begin to rotate the fingers inward...

4. Close up the posture by bringing the hands back to Bear position.

This is the Inside Change with the body opening and arms spreading out for just a moment, then closing down before you begin to walk in the opposite direction. Make sure you do not just open and close the arms but execute all movements with a twisting of the arms, from finger tips to shoulders

The Bear

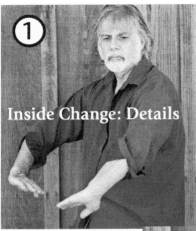

Inside Change: Details

1. To really do the Bear Turn correctly, you have to keep the word "shrug" in mind. Do not release the tension of the shrugged forward position during the transition process.

2. As you begin your turn to the left, open your arms by rotating both of them outward. The front of your chest may even expand a bit. At the same time, draw your arms away from one another and rotate them so the fingers face outward instead of pointing to one another.

3. As you complete your turn, rotate the fingers back in so they once again point to one another. Remember to roll your back and feel like you are pressing down toward the earth.

The Bear
Orientation: The body is turned a little beyond the center, about 30°.
Lead: Elbows
Associated Trigram: Ken, Keeping Still,
Represents Mountain
Body: The Upper Back and Kidneys
Medical: Gall Bladder

The Outside Change

The Outside Change is essentially the same as the Inside Change.

1. When you walk CCW, stop with your left (inner) foot forward.

2. Turn the left foot inward while twisting your body to the right. Open your arms and roll your chest as you turn. Your back is now to the circle

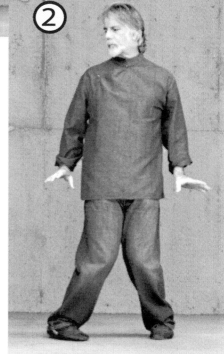

3. Continue rotating and open the right foot while you switch your gaze over your right shoulder. Just as you finish the change, close your arms back in the Bear's double downward arm twist.

The Bear

The Phoenix is known as FengHuang in Chinese. Feng is for the male, Huang for the female. The Feng is known as the ruler of the birds as the Dragon is known to be a universal ruler. Some Bagua practitioners substitute the Dragon for the Phoenix. The bent arms and wrists somewhat mimic the outspread wings of the Phoenix which glides through the clouds. Part peacock, part pheasant, part bird of paradise, the Phoenix is an explosion of colors. This mythical bird promotes duty, fidelity, responsibility and humanity; all qualities that match its smooth, gliding manner. The Phoenix is attuned to the Liver; in Chinese medicine this organ is associated with growth. The Gua or trigram it denotes is Chen or Thunder, often called the "The Arousing."

The Phoenix

This next animal is variously called the Phoenix or the Dragon in Bagua Zhang. This makes some sense if you remember that the Dragon is emblematic of the Emperor while the Phoenix is the special symbol of the Empress. Both of these are flying creatures. Both of them are also (and I hope this is news to no one) creatures that do not exist in the mundane plane of normal life. Being inhabitants of the imagination, we think of both creatures as being Yang energy, manifestations, products of the human mind.

Kung Fu sees other similarities between the Phoenix and the Dragon. The Dragon weaves through clouds, swimming as it were. This image of the dragon-movement, similar to the shape of the sine wave, represents all similar oscillating actions. In other words, "Dragon" is a short hand, a symbol, a template for a type of movement.

The Phoenix is much the same. Of the two, though they are both Yang, the Phoenix is the more Yin. The saying about her movement is that "The Phoenix traverses." She glides through the atmosphere as unhurried as a hawk, as unconcerned as a balloon. But her shape, in our Bagua exercise, is a bent, elbow-waving "w" somewhat like a zig zag turned up on its side. The Phoenix glides, the Dragon swims. The image of the swimming Dragon is so perfect for Bagua that some styles name themselves after it. Where the Dragon swims with vertical meandering, the Phoenix does the same, but horizontally.

The Phoenix introduces the first gesture where one arm is actually aimed away from the center of the circle. As you walk counter-clockwise the left (inner) one points toward the center. The arm is bent until the elbow is just about the height of the solar plexus.

Keeping the arm bent at this angle, the hand is held palm

facing directly upward. Of course, all of this is dependent on your personal limitations and flexibility. I will discuss modifications a little later. Try not to lift your shoulders as you walk. The other arm, the right, points exactly opposite the center of the circle so that both arms, if you are limber enough, from a radius pointing from center to Infinity. Because your arms are spread and bisecting the circle you will feel a digital difference between the rate of the hands as you walk. The rear right hand will seem to travel faster than the centered left hand and, indeed, its relative speed will be slightly greater since it points to the rim, not the hub, of the wheel.

Keys:

Either direction you walk with the Phoenix, you are facing toward the center of the circle. The tension of the neck muscles opening can put a little strain on you. The key is to keep the inside palm facing the centerpoint but also rotate the waist a little past the absolutely lateral. If you have the left hand pointing centerward, it's a good idea to rotate the waist a little extra to the Left so you have less strain on your neck muscles. At the same, time the outer hand—in this case the right—need not point exactly 180° opposite the circle center.

The Phoenix

The Phoenix Inside Change

1. Walk CCW then stop with the right (outer) foot in the lead.

2. Let both arms circle outward and away from your torso, fingers leading. As they fall, your arms will necessarily rotate inward.

3. As you continue the circle and rotate your arms past the comfort point, your hands will turn back into a Bear formation.

4. Bring the hands together in a prayer position. The timing of the feet will be exactly as before with the right foot rotating inward, then the left rotating outward to turn the body 180°, and point you in the Yang direction (CW).

5. Split the hands and reach out with them in the new Phoenix position facing the circle in a CW direction.

The Phoenix

The timing on this movement should emphasize the continued outward circling of the arms. The mid-point of the foot turning—right inward, left outward—should perfectly match the moment that the fingers first touch one another about the height of the Dan Tian.

The Phoenix Inside Change: Details

1. Walk with the Phoenix in the Yin (CCW) direction...

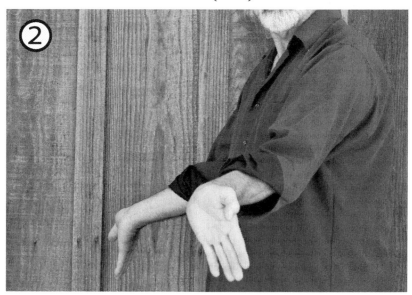

2. Start the change by following the fingertips as they circle outward and downward...

3. As your shoulders tighten you will naturally turn over your hands. Draw them together as though touching your fingers.

4. Continue bringing them into contact. When they touch, bring them up the front of the body in the prayer position.

5. Point outward with your fingers and open your arms into the Phoenix position. Continue walking the circle CW.

The Phoenix

The Outside Change:

Begin with the left (inner) foot in the lead. Turn your back on the circle and make sure you pass through the same sequence of postures that you did on the Inward Change.

1. Stop walking with left leg in the front.

2. Follow the fingers downward as the arms open out.

3. Turn in the left foot (kou bu) as your back faces the centerpoint. Your hands now resemble the Bear posture.

4. Keep turning right. Bring the hands together up your midline.

5. Turn out the right toes as your hands start to hook back and down.

6. Reach out and hook you wrists back while dropping your elbows. You have now reversed directions.

The Phoenix 71

The Phoenix
Orientation: The front fingers point directly to the center, the rear fingers point away but at an angle less than 180°.
Associated Trigram: Zhen, The Arousing, Represents Thunder
Body: The Elbows and sides of the ribs
Medical: The Liver Channel

Body Feel:

The Phoenix is said to focus energy on the elbows but we also say on the Liver. Speaking solely of the mechanical aspects, the elbows are well bent and also pressing downward. A second downward press is supplied by the backs of the wrists which are cocked and hooked, as though you were draping them over a bar and trying to push it downward.

If you do this with perfect symmetry you will indeed feel some pressure in the mid rib cage just about where the liver resides on the right side.

It's best to imagine both elbows pressing down on two circular rails as you walk. Don't strain though. Bringing too much tension into the neck or trapezius muscles is not productive. Since the Phoenix is focused on the Liver, and in Chinese medicine the Liver governs the tendons, think of the shape emphasizing strengthening the tendons rather than the muscles.

If you are performing the Half Breath Practice I showed you in the Snake section, you should completely relax and just steward the shape while walking. Then, in the other half of the circle walk, you would exhale, while pressing downward with about half your strength. As you press down, don't let it interfere with your walking. Slow and smooth still does the trick. This action of feeling the outer hand and inner hand rotating in relation to the Center should contribute to your feeling of gliding. Phoenix, as expressed in the bent elbows and articulated body position, should make you think of "folding" at each and every joint.

Her vantage point almost serene, the Eagle glides above the world, wings outstretched, her vision catching not only changes on the ground but peripherally between outspread wings. When swooping she manifests suddenly and catches her prey without halting her dive, just pulling up when she must, still calmly indifferent. Her wide gyre takes in everything, but is unaffected by anything. The Eagle, associated with the waist, is the master of turning and gliding, circling and diving. Eagle styles of Kung Fu also specialize in joint locks and throws (Chin Na and Shuai Jiao).

The Eagle

There is a basic saying in Bagua, that you should "change shape like the Eagle." As with many poetic phrases, this can be taken as just a nice image or a real piece of advice. The Eagle glides above the earth, riding the changeable currents of air. When she maneuvers from this vantage her moves are graceful, unhurried as her whole body adapts to the new shape. This graceful shape-changing is a very good habit to adopt, especially when you are learning fundamentals. As you progress in your Bagua education you will naturally speed up and even find yourself making the turns at blinding speed. For now, though, it is important to say how helpful it is to make each and every turn as slowly and effortlessly as possible.

Discussing the Eagle is a good time to clarify some ideas of Kung Fu practice which are often taken for granted, but rarely examined. Take the topics of softness and relaxation for example. The softness we strive for in martial practice has nothing to do with soft being better than hard. The real issue in soft training revolves around the nature of intrinsic and extrinsic movement. What makes Kung Fu a very different art from most is its emphasis on movements which are neither intrinsic nor intuitive. This doesn't make things easy by a long shot. When people move slowly and carefully, they do not revert to their intrinsic skills. Instead, they pay attention and, if they understand why they are slowing down, they will be surprised to learn how deep and profound slow motion can be. So be like an eagle and shift from shape to shape slowly and mindfully. The Eagle flies with its wings open and the walking pattern imitates this formation. This is the only posture in the basic animal movements where the arms completely overlap the outline of the circle instead of aiming at the centerpoint. The posture is very simple. When walking the circle counter-clockwise you spread your arms, palms up, out to the sides as though you were aligning them exactly on top of the edge of the circle itself. The only key point that you must control is to make sure that your arms are never separated by 180° or more. They must stay, at most, about 160° apart or you will over-rotate the shoulders and cause awkwardness in the movement.

The Eagle focuses attention on the waist. Walk the circle with your heart turned toward the centerpoint as much as possible. The arms outstretched along the circle act like two extenders augmenting the feeling of twist in the waist. You will feel a definite torque keeping them stretched like this.

Keys:
It is not easy to turn your heart directly toward the centerpoint of the circle, and you may find that, as you walk, you waver in and out of this position. Without using force, but keeping the concentration focused on your activity, you will learn that you can keep the shape of the movement without too much effort.

The Eagle scans the horizon as it hovers with the clouds. As it scans it keeps its eyes a bit unfocused, its gaze a little diffused. True, once it spots the rabbit or rodent its gaze tightens and telescopes down to a pinprick of intensity. When you walk the Eagle, you want to imagine that the lead hand is an opponent you are chasing down and the back hand is one chasing you. Keep them both in your peripheral vision at all times. Your are facing the centerpoint but you are not staring in that direction. Rather, your gaze takes in the extremities of both hand—pursuer and pursued—and expands your sense of the "rim."

There will be a distinct tendency for your back hand to fall down and morph into something other than good form. The bad boy in the class loves to lag behind and cause trouble. Try to FEEL that both hands are doing the same thing because, without that sense, you will have to divide your attention every moment to keep the form consistent. One easy answer is to lock the arms into one continuous bow, but this is not good Kung Fu. You want a connection between the arms because you keep that connection in your mind at all times, not because you mechanically linked them together and forget them. This is like drumming, not welding both hands together. Keep the idea of gliding and wheeling firmly fixed as you practice.

The Eagle Inside Change:

The Eagle has one extremely simple change and that is simply to turn your feet and walk in the opposite direction without changing your arms at all (unless you swing your waist hard in the new direction.) Unlike the other changes of the series though, this cannot be done for the Outside Change. To have a Palm Change that works Inside and Outward you need something completely different . . .

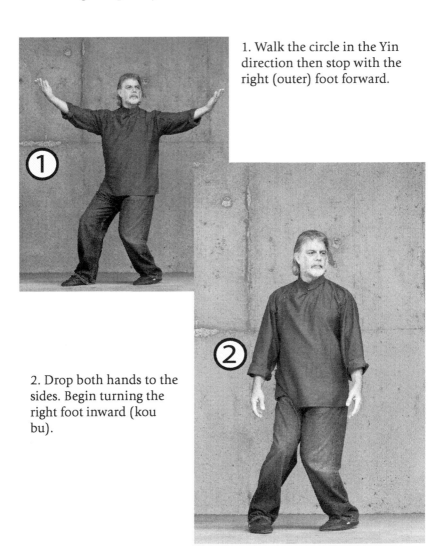

1. Walk the circle in the Yin direction then stop with the right (outer) foot forward.

2. Drop both hands to the sides. Begin turning the right foot inward (kou bu).

Bagua Zhang's Animals

3. As you continue turning to the left, raise both hands directly in front of you.

4. Finish the transition while opening both arms like wings. Walk in the new (Yang) direction, remembering to aim the heart to the centerpoint of the circle.

The Eagle 79

The Eagle Inside Change: Details

1. You are walking the circle CCW. Stop with the right foot in the lead.

2. Let both arms drop, swinging to your sides. The idea is to drop them as close as you can to your thighs (some practitioners actually brush their hands against their thighs just to make sure.)

3. Raise the arms, swinging them up so that both are at shoulder level with your left hand a little in the lead.

4. Separate your arms by opening them, especially the right arm stretching out in the CCW direction. Now walk the Eagle in the opposite (CW) direction...

The Eagle

The Outside Change:

This is a simple Eagle Change. You just throw down your arms then raise them as you complete the turn. *Note that in the aerial shot #3 I have already completed the rotation of the hands.*

1. Walking the Yin circle, you stop with the left (inner) foot forward.

2. As you turn left and place your back to the circle, you rotate your left toes inward (kou bu). Drop your arms comfortably to your sides.

3. Begin to raise both arms about shoulder width apart. As you continue to turn right, rotate your right toe outward (bai bu) as you go.

4. Just as you finish this action you will feel the extra force of opening both arms as you turn your waist and reverse direction on the circle.

The Eagle 83

The Eagle
Orientation: Try to turn the waist enough to point the heart to the center of the circle.
Associated Trigram: Sun, The Penetrating, Represents Wind and Wood
Body: The waist
Medical: The Belt Channel

A Different Outside Change:
(1.) Start walking the circle CCW, wings outstretched. When the left inside foot is in the lead, stop. (2.) Turn the left toe in. Keep the entire body in that position except for the left hand, which threads its way along the bottom of the right arm (3.) extending even beyond the right fingertips. When you feel the tremendous torsion in your waist, turn out your right toe and (4.) pull your right arm to the right and extend your left arm to the left while turning your body rightward and (5.) spinning around to face the centerpoint in the opposite direction.

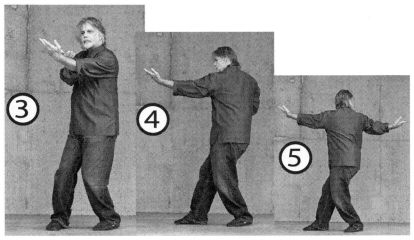

The Eagle   85

The Kite, or Sparrow Hawk, is a living bullet or, better still, a heat-seeking missile. He shoots through the forest barely avoiding making himself into bird pie by threading his way through the trees. But should he be startled by some ambitious creature, he changes course in an eye blink and shoots straight up between trees and into the overhead sky. The Sparrow Hawk is popular in Bagua because he represents the idea of threading through poles, opponents and other obstacles. In fact the style of Bagua I practice the most is known by the name Chuan Lin or Thread Through the Forest. Fast as lightning and as unstoppable as wind, the Hawk penetrates like a Kung Fu master's hands, slipping through an opponent's defense. The Sparrow Hawk corresponds to the heart.

The Kite (or Sparrow Hawk)

The Hawk Penetrating the Forest is a great image for Kung Fu, especially Bagua. A hawk streaks across our vision like horizontal lightning. We vainly scan to track his flight as he slices through the forest, seemingly without slowing. A ghost light flashing along a blade, he seems to cut through the trees, never stopping, veering and swooping. He captures our hearts with his speed and accuracy.

Many styles have a posture named after the hawk. In some ways, he perfectly symbolizes the Bagua art. Circling one instant he cuts an angle in midair as sharp as a sword slash. The circle is squared and the hawk energy takes his flight into the heart of the waving limbs, tree or human, without a blink of hesitation. In this version of the posture we not only have the hawk avoiding the trees but, on a sudden grand impulse, it shoots straight up into the sky. It moves as fast as an arrow aimed at the target moon. Hawk is a posture unique to itself, as you will see.

You walk the circle counter-clockwise, in the Yin direction.

Your Inner left arm is held high. The action of the left hand drilling upward will rotate the little finger side of the hand toward your face. In theory, you should be looking at the ulna side of the forearm as you walk, although the palm face will do. The placement of the shoulder is important everywhere in martial arts, but this posture needs a little more attention. Imagine your raised elbow right in line with your shoulders as though both shoulders form a straight line and the elbow lay on this line. Now move the elbow slightly, about an inch, inward from that line so there is a little bend in the front of the shoulder joint. That's fine. The right arm is placed pretty much as the normal guard position with the right forearm crossing the body and shielding the solar plexus. The fingers of the right hand droop toward the ground. The wrist is bent and relaxed, but not limp. It should look like you are flopping your right hand over an invisible bar. The actions of the two hands are in opposite directions. The upper hand drills upward. That's right, it doesn't just lift like your were holding up the ceiling. Instead, it should have the action of turning a light bulb clockwise as you elevate your arm. To balance this upward penetration, the lower hand not only hangs but actually performs a gentle downward pushing. The opposite yet complementary directional pressures of the hand should give you a feeling of "shearing." That is to say, the actions should make you feel as though you are lifting the left shoulder and dropping the right shoulder, like drawing a diagonal that crosses your torso.

The Sparrow Hawk or Kite
Orientation: The inner fingers point to Heaven, the outer hand fingers droop toward Earth.
Associated Trigram: Li, The Clinging
Represents Fire
Body: The upper front torso
Medical: Heart Channel

The Hawk Inside Change

1. Stop walking the circle CCW with the left hand high and the right foot in the front.

2. Now turn the right foot inward to the left in a kou bu. Begin dropping the left hand with a hooking smother move.

3. Complete the turn of the right foot while drilling up with the right hand from the inside.

4. Rotate your left foot outward. As you finish the reversal, drill upward with your right hand and press downward with the left hand.

5. With the drilling action completed, begin walking the circle in the Yang direction.

1. All you are going to do with the Hawk Change is to exchange the energies of the hands. The left hand begins to descend with the left elbow leading...

The Hawk Inside Change: Details

2. The right hand wants to rise and, to do that, it must immediately start to lift and aim the right index finger toward its goal (otherwise, the hands will clash.)

3. As the two hands pass in proximity, the right hand forms the upward drilling palm and the left hand allows the fingers to drop and become the draping hand with the left fingers pointing to the floor. The action of first turning in the right outer foot, then completing the transition with the left foot rotating outward, is the same as all other basic transitions.

4. Try to keep the action timed so that the midway point of the hand exchange is roughly the same as the mid-point of the body turn. Now you are walking the circle in the clockwise direction.

The Hawk

The Outside Change:

This is the same but, with your front side turning away from the circle. I continue to mention that these changes use the same simple footwork because I want you to see how much you can learn with a basic action, and how all animals may use, essentially, the same type of transformation.

1. Stop circling with the left (outer) leg in the lead.

2. Turn rightward, pivot inward with the left foot. Change your right hand to a fingers-up palm, and begin smothering with your left palm which faces the floor.

3. Continue turning. Bring the smother action down the outside of the rising right forearm. At this point you face away from the circle and both hands, one going up and one going down, should move at the same rate.

4, By the time your right hand has reached its zenith, your right toe should have moved out to align with the circle and your left hand should be in the palm down, fingers draped guard position.

The Hawk

The unicorn's actions relate to the stomach. Similar to the Snake, the hands are held about waist level. The front hand position is palm up but bent back so the fingers aim straight down toward the floor, with the palm facing the centerpoint. The rear hand is held with the palm facing inward, aimed toward the inner elbow of the front hand. The action of the Unicorn pulls back as though the top of your hand were hooking someone's wrist and dragging it toward your stomach. The rear hand presses towards but does not touch, the front arm's inner elbow. In the language of Chinese philosophy, this embracing and drawing movement represents the Earth

The Unicorn

The Unicorn of Chinese legend is quite a "different animal" from its Western cousin. First, the physical: The Chinese Unicorn is not a smooth, sleek-skinned white mare with a single polished bodkin for a horn. It is a mechanical contraption made from parts of lesser creatures resembling something like a Frankenstein nightmare (another horse of a different stripe.) Here is a list:

BODY of a deer.
TAIL of an ox.
HOOVES of a horse.
HORN, a fleshy stub, not a spike.

Other traits are less correspondent. For instance, its shaggy fur is multi-colored, except for its yellow-furred belly. The Unicorn (ChiLin or, in the Japanese language, "Kirin" if you recognize the beer) is always involved in magical situations. We follow Cheng Ho, the emperors' eunuch, who became the Chinese Christopher Columbus (except Cheng Ho did not exterminate the natives where he found them.) On a voyage to Africa he thinks he has found the Chi Lin.

Indeed the creature is yellow-furred, horse-hooved, nub-headed. Even the name GiRi (giraffe) in Somali resembles the Chinese word. So, back to Beijing and the Emperor Yong Lo, the commander returns with what he assumes is a wondrous present. But at first the Royal Court of the Forbidden City refuses to accept the gift. The offer of the present seems to indicate some incompleteness in the Imperial Entourage. But the Emperor's heart finally warms and the harmony is restored. It was believed that the Chi Lin appeared after momentous events had occurred. But it sometimes also stood in as a harbinger of profound change. Here is a young woman, Yang Zhen Zhai, months gone, looking out from her gate one day, startled to see a pair of dragons have come to guard the family compound. Then,

The Unicorn

later that same day, the symbol of the Earth—just as the dragons symbolized Heaven—comes trotting into the front court. It advances to the sitting mother-to-be, bends its forelegs, and makes the equivalent of a Unicorn courtesy. Next, it opens its mouth and unfurls the longest tongue one could imagine, a tree-wrapping tongue. As the tongue unravels, a tablet is revealed. The woman takes the tablet, calls for the house scholar, and receives the written message: "Here is a child that will be treated as an uncrowned king."

And that leaves us not only with a story that came true, as this mother of Confucius learned, but is remembered to this day among martial artists by the movement named "Unicorn Spits Book." The translation is a bit clumsy, perhaps we should say, "Unicorn Holds Jade Tablet in His Mouth." The association with the Earth, the feminine trigram, and the mother of them all, is also wrapped in the Chi Lin legend. For instance, the Unicorn will not devour any living creature. Even when it walks, it does not crush the grass. Like the earth, the Unicorn is fair to all. A famous judge, Kao Yao, was considered the icon of justice. Once he had decided a case though, he would invariably let the innocent free and administer justice by having the guilty stuck with a horn.

The Earth trigram for Kun, the Receptive

When we walk the circle, the outstretched hand bent backward against the wrist can be symbolic of the tongue that spat the prophecy of Confucius, or of the horn which made the "point" of Kao Yao's justice. The backward hooking action brings all things into the earthly embrace of the Unicorn.

Walking the circle counter-clockwise, you place your left, inner, palm facing the centerpoint. The palm is pulled back and down with the fingers pointing directly earthward. The palm itself points directly toward the center (assuming sufficient flexibility of your wrist). The inner, left, elbow points back to the stomach, the unicorn's organ of focus. There should be a separation of about a fist's thickness between the elbow and the

rib cage. The rear right palm faces the
inside of the left elbow. Its fingers are
gently pointing upward. Again there
should be about one fist's thickness
between elbow and palm.

The energy of the unicorn is that
of hooking backwards, towards the
stomach. Unlike the Snake, where the
hands are also held in one of the lower positions, the actions
of the unicorn actually pull away from the centerpoint. This
compression is also felt at the elbow tip where the elbow pulls
towards the stomach as though you were blocking with it. The
other hand presses toward the inner forearm without actually
touching it. This compression resembles holding a ball between
your right palm in the rear and the forward left elbow. The hand
actions which accompany this turn to the left are simple but
precisely timed. The right hand on the inside rotates to the palm
down position, something like Snake.

The Unicorn Inside Change:

1. The foot turning of this Inward Change is the same as in previous turns. The right foot steps to the front, and you halt your progress, still facing the center of the circle.

2. Turn the right foot inward with a kou bu or closed step. Start to smother downward with a palm-down pressing hand.

3. The right hand passes the left on the inside while the left descends

4. As the waist turns the body to the left, the left foot moves outward into a left bai bu open step. Now the right hand is lifting only to be...

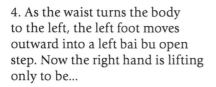

5. ...lowered with the back of the right hand and the bending of the right wrist. The left hand covers the inside of the right elbow.

1. The right foot steps to the front. From the position with the left palm aimed at the center of the circle...

The Unicorn Inside Change: Details

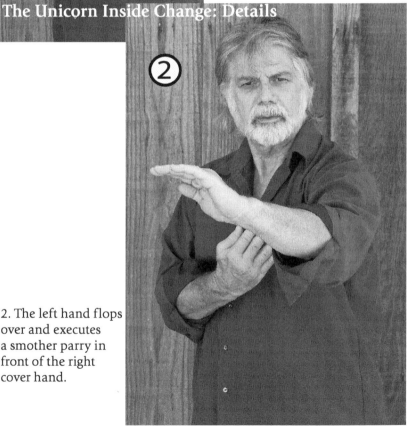

2. The left hand flops over and executes a smother parry in front of the right cover hand.

3. The right hand thrusts upward with the fingers pointing the way. Meanwhile the left hand is still rotating and smothering.

4. As you complete the turn, the right wrist bends back and hooks downward. By now the left hand has taken up its position behind the right elbow. The foot turning and the hand exchange should complete at the same moment.

The Outside Change:

1. When the left foot is in the lead on the counter-clockwise circle...

2. you start turning your back to the centerpoint while elevating the left hand...

3. The left hand flips over, palm down, smothering downward. The left toe turns inward.

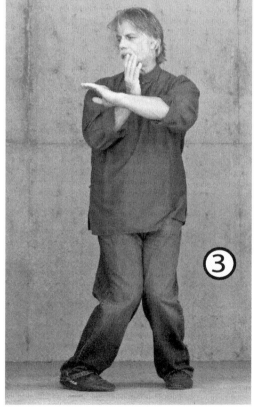

4. Somewhat in the manner of the Hawk, the right hand thrusts up and through the circle created by the descending smother of the left hand. The right toe turns out (bai bu).

5. The right hand flips palm up and follows the arc of the left ending with the fingers downward, the palm facing centerpoint. The action of the hands should be continuous and sequential like cascading water. The second hand always reaches out then falls over like a huge lapping tongue.

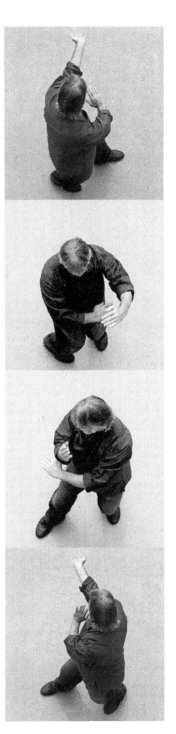

The Unicorn
Orientation: The inner palm faces the center. The palm of the back hand faces the inner elbow.
Associated Trigram: Kun, The Receptive
Represents Earth
Body: The stomach
Medical: Stomach Channel

Keys:
The action of the Unicorn concentrates on an essential of all martial practice including western boxing and wrestling, namely, the relationship between the elbows and the rib cage or stomach. There should be a constant bond between them, invisible but tactile. The elbows need not touch the ribs but the martial artist has a constant sense of the possible need to drop the elbow into a strong defensive position. Therefore, as you walk, you will want to feel this strong linkage between the elbow and the ribs. This imaginary compression should emphasize the "stomach" aspect of the training which often feels as though you were pushing something into your stomach and tensing it a little.

Elements:
The Unicorn is synonymous with the Earth trigram, just as the Lion correlates to the Heaven gua. Earth also pairs, in Chinese medicine, with the stomach which is in many ways, the center of metabolic activity in the human body. When walking the circle the player practicing Unicorn should keep almost constant, though slight, pressure on his stomach. A little tension, a little waist turn, a definite hooking action back toward the body.

The Unicorn, because it is concentric and downward, gives you a strong sense of walking around a real centerpoint. You feel the definite pull toward the middle.

An old Chinese medical saying has it that, "Monkeys never cough because they are always moving their shoulder blades." And, indeed, the mischievous Monkey seems to love activity, movement and getting into trouble. The Monkey is constantly curious and loves to peek into hidden corners. His deep set eyes only allow him to look straight so he must constantly move his head to alter his angle of vision. Climbing, jumping, spinning, the Monkey is the most agile of the Bagua creatures. In some ways he represents change itself. Monkey forms of Kung Fu, including Bagua, emphasize strong legs, deep stances, agile movements, indirect attacks and swift changes. The Monkey's symbol from the I Ching is the Youngest Daughter (Dui), a manifestation of Joy which, in the case of the Monkey, may mean mischievous joy.

The Monkey

We think of the monkey as Kung Wu Song, the immortal Monkey King so beloved by the Chinese. Mischievous, brilliant, war-like but playful, the Monkey King annoyed all the inhabitants of heaven by stealing the peach of immortality. In BaGua, he offers that same peach to you in a signature movement known as Ape Offers Fruit. Nice as it seems, you must exercise a little care as this offer of fruit may also be the prelude to climbing right up your arm and sitting on your head.

The monkey embodies the trait of Lin, or Agility. His actions are to reach out and then contract tightly. This latter is emphasized initially in the movements of the Monkey circling exercise. As you will see, both sides of the monkey, —extend and withdraw—are represented in the application of his talents.

The Monkey is the last animal of the series and arguably the most compact, with the arms held tight almost touching the body. The energy of the monkey HAS to be agile because, though the size of the circle is the same as with the other animals the monkey movements have a natural tightness to them which may make you feel like you are chasing your own tail.

In its most basic and fundamental form, the Monkey walks the circle with both arms held right in front of the chest. The palms face straight up to heaven, the elbows droop straight down to the earth. The hands are held approximately chin high with the little fingers side of both hands aimed at the circle, and the fingers themselves almost facing in opposite directions. The distance both elbows and hands are held away from the body should be about the width of a fist but, of course, you must modify each stance for personal limitations such as flexibility.

The forearms are almost touching with about two fingers breadths between them. The waist turns so much that the heart and the lungs (the corresponding area of the Monkey posture) are aimed as much as possible toward the centerpoint.

The Monkey is a posture that looks almost perfectly symmetrical but, when you are actually **doing** the movement of the Monkey, it feels nothing like this. This is because the Monkey hand position, which looks like a sunflower facing high noon, is also a twisting action. As you point your palms upward you also turn them in the same direction in which you walk the circle. You walk, say, counter-clockwise and you simultaneously turn both palms in the same direction with the hands making a smaller circle parallel to the larger one on the ground. Sometimes the directional component feels so strong you may actually experience being pulled around the bend.

The second component of the Monkey is a slight but persistent forward pressure toward the circle interior. Think of taking the little finger sides of your hands and pushing them toward the centerpoint. As you walk, hold "offer the fruit" and try to make that offering pressure as constant as you can. It won't be easy.

You may find, here more than in most of the other animals, that the Monkey posture is affecting the way you walk. You can see why this is so. Your arms are held together so close that your chest is closed down. You are twisting tightly with the hands as though turning a very small wheel. Your steps will be affected, and all that signifies is that you are starting to really perform Bagua, allowing it to alter your whole body with the spiraling energy of the art.

The Monkey
Orientation: The space between the forearms is aimed at the center.
Associated Trigram: Dui, The Joyous
Represents Lake
Body: The chest area
Medical: The Lung Channel

The Monkey Inside Change:

For most people, the Monkey is one of the most difficult turns. Perhaps that is why it was put at the tail end of the series. There is, however, an easy version. The only problem is that it may seem **too** easy.

1. You are walking the circle CCW. When your right foot is in the lead, start to turn to the left.

2. As you turn, hold your arms frozen in exactly the same relationship to your body. Turn the right toe inward.

112   *Bagua Zhang's Animals*

3. Continue the turn and allow the hands to drift across your center line as you open your left toe (bai bu).

4. As the turn is completed, rotate your hands back toward center with a slight wrist rotation to the right. In this Change you do very little with your hands, just slightly compensate for the turning of the body. Just allow them to turn slightly in the direction of your waist movement.

The Monkey Inside Change: Details

1. From the CCW direction...

2. Turn the body and rotate both hands to the back. As you do this you should feel some contraction in the chest and a corresponding opening of the back.

3. When you start walking to the CW direction...

4. rotate the edges of the hand back toward the centerpoint.

The Inside Change, Alternate:
A slightly different way of performing the turn has you starting the rotation with the wrists **before** you turn your feet. In both cases the feet perform the right foot closing and the left foot opening exactly as with all the other basic turns. But the hands immediately start rotating to the left just like a little cog in a machine and your body follows, aligning itself with that action. Suddenly there you are, turned in the other direction.

Keys:
The focus of the Monkey movement is the lungs. The very act of imitating the monkey should cause this feeling of compression. That's why it is important that you don't just relax your shoulders and touch your forearms against one another. In other words, don't just use your arms to bring them together; instead the closing of the arms should be the <u>effect</u> of the back opening and the chest closing. The correct action renders the arms essentially passive.

The Monkey is the most radically twisted of all the animals. You want to feel a lot of torsion in the waist but don't use strength or force and actions. The main emphasis is on a constant centripetal force. The more you open the fingers, the more you will feel the pressure of the movement in your hands. Try to actually straighten out your fingers and continue to imagine you have a huge peach in your hand which you are turning constantly while you eat it and walk the circle.

The Outward Change:

1. When turning outward, just start twisting the hands in the new direction and let the left foot follow.

2. Continue without interruption until you are completely facing away from the circle.

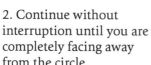

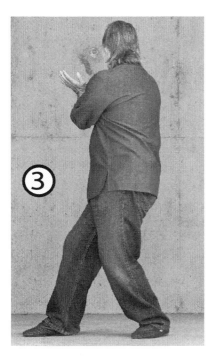

3. Finish the change by opening the right foot and continuing to rotate the chest until you have reversed position.

The Monkey

An Alternative Change: Details

You will probably regret reading this one. Showing you this is like handing one of those little ball games to you, the kind you waste hours trying to beat. This is an alternative change utilizing what is known in Kung Fu as a Flower Hand. The forearms do not move much more than in the easy change, but the hands...

1. Stop walking the Monkey posture with the right leg forward.
2. Roll the left hand, palm down, over the right, the thumb edge moving toward your nose. Turn the right hand palm upward.
3. Continue this CW movement as you roll your left hand palms forward and upward. The right hand reaches to the front and begins to follow the rotation of the left hand.
4. Continue rotating, bringing first the left then the right fingers past your face.
5. Move them to the left side of the body. It you have shifted your feet properly you are now ready to walk in the opposite direction.

The Philosophy of Change

(The following section discusses the art of Bagua Zhang as it relates to the wider picture of Chinese philosophy and the underlying principles of Yin and Yang. Though not necessary to a study of the art, it offers an introduction to the origins of this martial practice.)

The I Ching is a profound Chinese book that has been around for thousands of years. It proposes that Change is always with us, regardless of how it is clothed. We can never exactly know the shape and shadow of unlit dawns, but as they clear and turn to day we can modify our lives accordingly. Every moment offers us a new turn in the stream, and the I Ching is meant as a guide to show us how to pick the right stepping stones to cross that stream with a minimum of danger.

This ancient idea of adapting to change is so deeply ingrained in Chinese culture that it is like the water surrounding the fish, so familiar that few even notice it. The I Ching and the wisdom it offers has been, to the Chinese, as wide-spread and significant as Christianity has been in Western culture.

As a product of that culture, the martial art of Bagua Zhang took the I Ching as its platform. Bagua Zhang practice starts with Yin and Yang. Yin represents a quality receptive, yielding, fluid and formless. Yang, its complement, represents everything in the universe that is creative, firm, stable and definitive. These are the two building blocks of the I Ching and, since Yin and Yang cannot be separated, they form a pair called the Liang Yi or Twin Influences.

Bagua Zhang embraces this philosophy by concentrating on all types of paired changes that arise from the interplay of Yin and Yang. Every one of these originates with the Liang Yi, the combination of these twin influences. When you walk the circle you have an inside hand and an outside hand. You walk clockwise or counter. You determine change by the outside leg or the inside leg. You inhale and exhale to practice Qigong. You mix soft and hard, fast and slow, large and small.

In addition to recognizing the importance of the Liang Yi, the Chinese believe that all this interplay of Yin and Yang occurs in a three-leveled world. The top layer is said to represent Heaven, the bottom Earth and the middle level Mankind, forever caught between Heaven and Earth.

A three-level symbol made up of Yin or Yang lines is called a trigram, or GUA, in Chinese. There are only eight possible combinations of Yin and Yang and each of these trigrams manifests a special quality. For instance a bottom line that is Yang with two Yin lines above it represents Zhen or Thunder. The

ancients believed that thunder originated in the earth like a strong Yang line breaking through. Since Thunder startles, the trigram was also named "The Arousing." Or imagine two Yin lines with a Yang on top and you have the symbol for Stillness and the image of a mountain hollow with caves but standing immobile as eternity.

The name of our art is Ba (Eight) Gua (Trigrams) Zhang (Palm). The word "palm" here means a form of Kung Fu, so we can translate the name as Eight Trigrams Kung Fu or Eight Trigrams Boxing.

Change like this is reflected in every aspect of Bagua practice. Defense effortlessly turns into attack. Striking becomes grappling in a blink. By skillfully turning this way or that, clockwise or counter-clockwise, the Bagua stylist turns the force away from himself, redirecting it into complete dispersion or even back into the opponent.

Each martial art has a specialty. Some emphasize strength and stability. Some have only a few key moves. Bagua meets conflict with the idea of change. Where some arts stress stability, Bagua emphasizes mobility. Where almost all martial studies start with relatively static steps, Bagua begins with continual, fluid foot patterns.

When you study Bagua, it is good to keep in mind its history and its principles. The practice of the Eight Animals is a good example. Each animal has a fixed upper body position. This represents the underlying principles of Bagua: while you walk the circle constantly changing the upper body retains its shape by adapting. Here is the reality of Bagua in an ever-changing world. It is the interplay between the constantly moving feet and the fixed but subtly adjusting upper body that brings you right into the act of managing Yin and Yang. To move constantly, and yet keep a particular point in view, requires this management, this harmonizing of many elements.

The Eight Trigrams:
Earth, Mountain, Water, Wind,
Thunder, Fire, Lake & Heaven

Bagua and Qigong

You start with a few circles, just walking as casually as you would in your garden in the morning. Then you lift your hands in one of the animal positions and, as you walk, allow your breath to relax. After a while, your entire body loosens up; ropey, relaxed but with a keen focus as though you had cleaned your windows. You may move this way or pause your walk for a minute. When you stand there, you continue the even, fluid breathing. Your arms gradually loose their weight and almost float toward the sky. Your breath descends and you feel yourself gently stretched, as though your entire spine were the string tied to a helium balloon…

Qigong is a very ancient method of relaxation, inhalation and physical exercise. It is also a method for tap ping into a meditative state. The principle behind qi practice is that there is a vital energy, something like bio-electrical energy, coursing through the human body. Qigong, among other things, attempts to regulate this flow and to ensure the continued natural functioning of qi. In recent years it has become something of a craze, but most of the major concepts and practices are still unknown to most people.

There is an entire branch of Qigong that is practiced by martial artists. This is considered a higher level than most Qigong practice available to the public. In fact, Qigong has benefited greatly by all the experiments and special conditions of martial practice through the centuries. Often martial Qigong is all that is necessary for a perfectly rounded and beneficial practice.

The question is, should you practice Qigong? Let's say that you don't have any present complaints. Why practice something which most people, at least in the modern world, associate with some kind of respiratory therapy? You may already be familiar with some of its well-known benefits such as relaxation, postural integration and beneficial contributions to conditions such as insomnia, depression and high blood pressure. But do you need to practice it?

The answer is that Qigong can benefit almost anyone with its relaxing, normalizing benefits, but martial arts students get a bonus. Qigong training is one of the best methods to relax the body into the framework of your studies. In fact, the animals were designed as Qigong postures, perfectly tailored for Bagua practice. They can strengthen you, correct your structural alignment, make new and uncomfortable positions into comfortable ones, help you to develop lightning quick reactions and, over all else, combine this practice of Bagua Zhang with the health benefits of Chinese medicine. In the simplest terms, adding Qigong to your practice is like adding a free acupuncture treatment to each workout session!

How Qigong Works

People wandering into Tai Chi or Qigong studios are taught a bunch of loose hand waves and some simple breathing methods. Sometimes they feel benefits from this practice. Often they stop training, having never really understood what they were doing in the first place. They were told to move their hands around, stand in strange positions, and imagine rays of light. But they are often completely ignorant of the mechanics of Qigong.

So let me introduce you to some of the mechanics right now. The great thing is that if you have tried to play with the Bagua animal postures, you are already doing some Qigong.

The first rule is just common sense. Most people cannot, just by will power, isolate their internal organs such as their liver. Contrary to the kind of wishful-thinking approach some Qigong teachers take, there has to be a method and the method is obvious but essential. When you have a stomach ache you bend over and grasp your stomach. When you wake up and want to g the day you may spread your elbows and stretch your back. External physical movement has a natural correlate to internal conditions. Qigong takes this idea considerably further. We know, for instance, that physical movement of the external body can build internal muscles, especially if we use resistance. But if you want to go even deeper you must relax those muscles so the torque created by the actions of your limbs bypasses muscular tension and is transferred directly to the organs. This is the hydraulics of Qigong practice.

Once a well "sealed" posture has been established every cc of breath that you inhale adds internal pressure to the region of interest. In other words once the tube has been twisted into a certain shape, pumping air through it can redirect considerable pressure. This is the pneumatics of Qigong.

Can you see why waving your arms around and visualizing blue light is not particularly effective, except for those souls already slanted toward that fantasy? I do not say this to make fun of people, but as a reaction to a view that Asian thought is essentially metaphoric and poetic without any real intelligence and experience. This condescending attitude, that thousands of years of qi research is roughly equivalent to someone's daydreams, is itself an insult to a great civilization, one that excelled in science and mathematics when Europe was mostly mud.

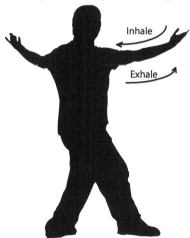

Each and every one of the animal postures is meant to direct vectors of torque specifically to the unseen interior of the body. The limbs play a crucial part in this activity. The legs must not only be stable, but must have the kind of tension that reinforces the action of the arms. The arms, which are far more variable, position themselves to direct this force very selectively to regions in the body. The lines of torque follow the traditional channels of the body associated not just with acupuncture but with all of Chinese medicine. Thus the shape of the body is the shape of the qi. Like a great river it can be partially redirected through the internal environment to irrigate areas previously suffering from draught or flooding.

The Bagua player must be able to stretch a hand out to any angle or relationship he has caused in his twisting, spinning and whirling movements. His shape-changing—for that is what it is—will manifest with arms twisting backwards, elbows inverted, palms pressing in opposing directions, and limbs coiling around themselves like snakes in a washing machine.

The foundation for all this is the Eight Animals practice. Each arm position creates a special Qigong posture. And all you have to do to begin this practice is stop, stand in one of the animal postures, and concentrate on your breathing. Try this and taste the unique flavor of each of these dynamic postures.

The Spirit of Bagua

The physical exercise of martial arts is a form of fighting gravity, yet embracing gravity. In the long tradition of martial training it became clear that the art lay in the legs, the roots, the connection to the earth. Many methods try to ground the student by having him stand in a low position, often with legs sizzling on fire and sweat streaming like a jiggling teapot. Then there are long sessions of just shifting back and forth, slowly transforming one's lower body into this shape and that, each of these shapes a momentary configuration like sand wetted by an outgoing wave.

When you practice Tai Chi your spirit is grounded, relaxed and loose. Power consolidates in you like paper stacked and compressed in thousands of sheets which collectively achieve the strength of steel.

Bagua also starts with the roots. Bagua also has an approach all its own but with the spirit held higher. The requirement of walking the circle does not always fit well with a Tai Chi-like downward setting. In Bagua the spine lifts heavenward and the body spins along this spine. The external resemblance to the "Whirling Dervishes" is obvious. Rumi's sacred Medlevis spin continuously, tombstone caps pulled tight to resist the centripetal force as they break through to the world of mystic truth.

The Bagua practitioner may not know it but he, too, is tied to a spiritual practice, that of the Black Hat sect of Daoism. This meditative circumambulation was a key practice of this group known throughout the world for its knowledge of Feng Shui. Akin to their twirling cousins—just as Daoism is surprisingly akin to Sufism—the black hat disciples walked the circle to help them enter a meditative state.

You should do the same. The first effect of the walking is that you must release the connection to looking fixedly in any direction. As you walk you must also remember your root, your feet. But that, too, differs from so many martial studies, in Bagua you are not allowed to stand for a moment. You must step and plant, step and plant; never ceasing while your eyes glide across reality.

You will feel a bit of a battle at first, when eyes and feet suddenly act as though they can no longer communicate with one another. How incredibly clever of the Bagua masters to attack a relationship so ingrained and so assorted. The birth of art and mysticism and, yes, science is the moment we cease taking the ordinary as the ordinary.

The spine comes into its own here: an erect (but not stiff) central pillar actually connected at one end to the pedestal of the pelvis, at the other to peering eyes. We keep the spine upright so the two eyes scanning the self-created horizon are secure. At the same time we keep the spine loose enough so that the inexact, often tentative, stepping aberrations—now a collection of stalls and rushes—are not transmitted to the head too strongly. The spine acts as a shock absorber, as does the constant twist in the neck favoring one side or the other.

Erect, flexible, light and constant. The spirit of Bagua seems very distant as befits a Chinese martial style. The thing about Bagua, about circling, about constantly returning, is that if your attention slips, your foot hesitates, your mind skips, your eyes wander; if anything untoward occurs, you just keep going and, lo and behold, you have circled to the same spot again and another chance to try and perfect your movement. Bagua never halts for regrets.

Changing Perspective, Perceiving Change
Walking a circle turns things around. There's little chance to rest and if, you bend your knees enough, you will work up a considerable sweat. But much of the effort is mental and your constant attention eventually realizes it is attention itself that undergoes a radical transformation.

I don't think it would take a course in Jungian psychology for most of us to admit the archetypal, architectonic and just plain rightness of the circle as a form. Chesterton said, "Three perfect things are circles: a baby's bottom, a marriage ring and eternity." The connection of the circle reminds us of many profound things both personally and in the long history of humans. It does not surprise that dervishes (and often Hasidim) circle in their spirit-drunken ecstasies. The halo is a simple but wonderfully apt symbol of perfected humanity. The teacup, if you are one of us tea lovers, brings to mind a horizon in safe harbor, of a world complete. The stars travel in circles (ellipses being not inferior in their perfection by one jot.) The congruence of the smallest electron orbit to a whirling galactic center reminds us not only of Einstein's profound insight that space is curved but that, since it is so shaped, everything in space must be circling in one way or another.

Yes, if we consider the breadth of reality—not from the often-employed perspective of a Martian but, on a grander scale, from the perspective of a stranger from an entirely different reality—we would, with the shock of recognition unsuspected, have to admit that the particular reality we share with all the universe is almost entirely circles, and circle and circles. This clockwork universe clicks and ticks, joined with wheels and gears intimately entwined; visible and hidden; fundamental and ornamental, simultaneously.

Our human ancestors brought the line into creation. We build our houses square and hack direct, amazingly straight, roads through the Yucatan jungle. Trigonometry preceded spherical coordinate systems by hundreds of years, just as it should have, for if Euclid had considered the possibilities of a circular world so early in history, "The Elements" would probably never have been written.

The old civil contention of the sacred and the profane—

the human mind and the animal nature; the artful and the innocent—also finds an intriguing contest in the circular and the straight. (The fact they are inseparable and actually the same thing I will arrive at eventually, circularly of course). Our muscles rotate, our minds spin, but our eyes pierce and our wills drive straight forward. We are a confusion of angles and sweeps.

Our machine-created society has corralled us into moving in a new way, at least new with regard to human history. This is evident in the practice of teaching traditional martial arts where students often complain, "That move doesn't feel natural to me." After hearing this for years I finally decided to inquire, "Which moves do feel natural?" I was surprised at their frankness as they mentioned or acted out driving, or typing, or turning a door knob in every case some series of actions where the human body has adapted itself to machines; their angles, tracks and grooves.

So you can expect some change of consciousness as you practice this art, especially in the early stages. First and most obvious will be dizziness. Dizziness doesn't just evaporate but it does slowly transform into something much more manageable with continued practice.

Walking the circle first requires a sense of the relationship between the foreground and the background. The foreground is most commonly the sight of your own hand stuck out there between your nose and the center of the circle. The background exists not there, but beyond the rim of the circle unless interrupted by a pole or other object. At first when you walk, the outside world seems to spin at the speed of a carousel. Look in the Q&A section for ideas on how to control your dizziness.

Coming Full Circle

Never Too Clearly

Confucius said, "Never explain too clearly". His idea was obvious and true. The student has to invest something of herself in the learning process or she won't really and truly learn. Bagua doesn't need much confusion added to the mix, however, because its subtle nature already requires a lot of student participation.

Bagua Zhang, in this regard, is a breakthrough concept. Like a modern hologram, it contains a great deal more "information" than most other styles. It has the rare attribute of concentrating the information without expanding the structure of the style proportionately. What does this mean? Well its movements are folded or, one might say twisted, into one another so that—in essence— each Bagua move is the equivalent of ten other movements from "normal" martial arts.

Take the core movement of Bagua itself, the Drilling Palm. You lift your hand, fingers upward, as you spiral the forearm and twist the fingers in a drilling action that sends your arm upward, cleaving to centerline like a razor blade. In application, you are blocking a punch. The punch strikes the rotating radial section of your forearm and spins off to the outside of your arm. But wait. Let's consider a replay: the punch is blocked by the other side of the forearm, and the same spinning motion, without alteration, spins the oncoming punch off to the other side of the forearm. It's like throwing beans at a spinning electric fan blade. If one bean hits one side it spins off in one direction. Another bean hitting the other side spins off in the opposite direction. And here's another replay: the expected punch never reaches the forearm (perhaps it was a feint). Instead, you drive your spinning hand forward toward the opponent's throat in an uninterrupted spear hand strike. Replay: OR the opponent grabs your wrist and, to counter the grab, you rotate your forearm to torque the opponent's arm and twist his wrist free of the grasp. In yet another replay, you counter grab and snap the wrist.

<u>In every case, you performed the same movement.</u>

Remember that meditation, art and martial studies occupied healthy amounts of Chinese genius for many centuries. As knowledge and experience accrued, much of martial genius became allusive, a hint at a well-known reference just as the six words "to be or not to be" bring the entire realm of a ruminating Denmark to mind. Bagua is an art of allusions; a mere gesture can become a block, strike, grapple or throw on the practical level, and a thing of art, an aid to Qigong, a mudra, or a method of strengthening or stretching. Everything is folded, not to be obscure or subtle but to save the serious martial artist time, to immediately plant him in the arena of SIGNIFICANT martial studies, not the kindergarten of high kicks and simple motions we so often see.

A good example of this idea is the animals themselves. Not only does each animal have specific movements for self-defense that rely on its nature, but each animal has a number of such qualities. Following is a list of the striking, grappling and other "skills" of each animal. Even when these strikes, such as "chopping," are duplicated in the lists, they are executed differently within the style of each particular animal.

Bagua Zhang's Animal Techniques

Not only does each animal have specific movements for self defense that rely on its nature, but each animal has a number of such qualities. Here is a list of the striking, grappling and other "skills" of each animal. Some of these strikes such as "chopping" are duplicated in the lists but executed with the style of a particular animal.

Lion: Smashing, sweeping, hooking, chopping, grasping, seizing, cutting and blocking.

Snake: Hip, knee, elbow, shoulder, holding, winding, shooting and grasping.

Bear: Rushing, withdrawing, penetrating, leaning, carrying, shocking, softening and following.

Phoenix: Chopping, entering, moving, capturing, carrying, leading, pushing and lifting.

Eagle: Stabbing, curling, removing, transforming, shocking, extending, dodging, chopping.

Hawk: Shifting, dodging, extending, lifting, entering, rushing, stabbing and whipping.

Unicorn: Following, kneading, sticking, softening, hip, chopping, cutting and striking.

Monkey: Chopping, winding, hip, stomping, popping, stamping, swinging and cutting.

Bagua's Nature

The nature of Bagua is elusive, in more ways than one. There are those who think Bagua's supreme tactic is just a way of running around behind the other fellow like an eight-year old trying to out-fox a giant. But the broader strategy is an attempt to entice the other fellow into your Bagua world because, unless he has studied Bagua, he does not stand a chance in that world.

The nature of Bagua is also deceptive. "The art of war is the art of deception," wrote Sun Tzu in the world's most famous manual on military strategy, "The Art of War." Why should the martial artist be any different than a military commander? We should always distinguish between the truly martial—that is to say, military-based styles—and personal combat arts. Northern Chinese Kung Fu styles, for example, are military-based. They were invented to be used on the battlefield as well as for personal protection. In fact, the often obsessive concern of modern people, personal safety, was not a primary concern of the ancient martial artists; victory was. The martial artist of the past was there to kill the other soldier, not protect his own life. For a soldier, the very best protection is to not go to war in the first place, but that wasn't an option. To quote a prominent teacher and scholar, Adam Hsu, "Martial arts was not meant to beat the opponent. It was meant to destroy him." In fact martial artists of 1000 years ago often learned weapons skills before, and sometimes completely instead of, empty-handed maneuvers. As the cold weapons—instruments like spears and swords—gradually marched off the field, hot weapons such as cannons entered to dominate the arena; and from that point martial arts changed, never to be the same again.

Bagua is a late addition. It is one of the last truly classical styles to be created and it has taken many ideas from its predecessors. It has brought military strategy down to the personal combat level, keeping its emphasis on deception, evasiveness, change and adaptation. It has incorporated many weapons and steeped all of them in the Bagua flavor. It has absorbed most of the striking, locking and throwing tactics from the entire Kung Fu arsenal.

If Bagua were to be pinned down as a school of military strategy it would live in the art of guerrilla fighting. For instance, Bagua relies on the principle that **force should not be squared off against force**. This is a famous martial dictum followed in many styles of Kung Fu with many different ways to execute it. Bagua Zhang's sophisticated methods center on the use of angular relationships. In truth, this can be found in ALL forms of combat. A good practitioner can "cut the corners", not just striking at seemingly impossible angles but even thinking with unique angles. Sometimes the angular deviation is huge, sometimes it is barely visible, perhaps only perceivable by the poor unfortunate just before pain explodes in his body.

One of the things that makes Bagua unusual is that it suggests—no, demands—that you make the transition to this type of thinking from Day One. That is why we call Bagua a "black belt" art: it starts with ideas which often take years of training in other arts. Bagua is a study where even the most basic act, walking the circle for instance, completely changes the way you consider what might formerly have seemed a rather obvious action. In Bagua, you take the everyday act such as moving your hand from point A to point B and FIND the twisting hidden in that motion. The more you study Bagua, the more you realize that you have been approaching a spiral world with a straight line mentality. Bagua reveals the "grain" in every growing thing, in every natural motion. It is a perfect style to help you realize how robotic and unnatural most movement in the modern human world really is. This gives the Bagua practitioner a freedom unique in martial arts. No one knows just how much twist YOUR body is capable of, or how many folds YOUR mind can see in any given movement. Therefore it follows that YOUR Bagua will be different from mine. Contrary to what many people think about martial arts, this customization process has always been an ingredient of true martial studies. Rarely has any style offered it so early in the student's career, and with such art, strength and beauty.

Questions and Some Answers

Q: What if I get dizzy when I walk?
A: The question is not "if," but "when". Some moment, regardless of how seemingly unaffected you are, you WILL get dizzy. Of course you can stop the practice any time you want, catch your breath and your balance. There are also some things you might investigate just to see if they have anything to do with vertigo. But when you continue, you will first have the question of where to aim your gaze. The easy answer is to try everything. Most commonly, people who stare at their own hands often find themselves getting dizzy. The contrast between the relatively stable hand and that whirling background outside the rim of the carousel is just too stark. One strategy you might try is to soften your focus just as you might do with a camera lens, and allow the background and foreground of your vision to blur a bit.

Some people have concentrated on the hands, at the same time, half on the scenery. They report good results with this strategy.

One interesting sidebar is that the distance between the practitioner and the object of his focus can relate to dizziness. For instance, Bagua has an exercise where two people walk touching each other and very close together, less than eighteen inches from one another. People who have never been dizzy before, become dizzy on this one. I remember being curious about this so I paid particular attention to my students and noticed that when they walked that close to one another they tended to lean away from their partners, either maintaining a distance for clarity of vision or, just as likely, a social buffer. When I had them keep absolutely straight while walking, and stare PAST their partners, much of the dizziness disappeared. The same would be true for walking really close to a pole while trying to focus your eyes on it. Never fear, walking and experimenting with your focus will resolve your dizziness.

Q: Is Bagua performed slowly, like Tai Chi. I had heard it was done really fast?
A: Bagua has a progression of skills and requirements, the same as Tai Chi. In the case of Bagua, the Palm Changes are

generally performed very slowly. Walking the circle is performed at roughly average or comfortable speed, but when the change appears you should slow down and squeeze all the juice out of it. As you progress, you should increase the walking speed and gradually work toward a significant speed increase in the execution of the changes. The reason for this is that speed tends to show you the efficiency, or lack of it, in any Bagua movement. The closer you get to full speed, at least in occasional practice, the more you realize that there are very few wasted moves in Bagua. But speed acquisition should be comfortable and just as gradual as you need.

Q: When I try to increase my speed everything gets jerky.
A: This is indeed the danger of trying to improve your speed. Another problem can be that everything seems sloppy. There's an old saying in CMA that "Slow is fluid, and fluid is fast." It is not the paradox it seems. Slow gives you the correct and most efficient pathways to move. Once you have these, speed is inevitable.

Q: What about Bagua weapons?
A: This is somewhat outside the scope of this book but a few brief comments might be useful. The vast majority of Bagua weapons forms are Shaolin style forms that have been altered to fit Bagua, or they are Bagua weapons forms developed in relatively recent times. There's nothing wrong about this, but I have to say that not all of them are up to top standard. In addition to the classical weapons such as the straight sword and staff, there are some exotic weapons such as the Elk Horn Knives and the Judge's Needles. Given their unique attributes, these are so perfectly fit for Bagua that they actually help you develop your empty handed skills. Bagua is a totally integrated martial system. When you are working on the hand forms you are learning the basics of the weapons with very little translation needed.

Q: I find the walking very complicated and difficult to practice for a long time. Any suggestions?
A: People are often surprised at first how much work it is to walk this way. But of course it gets easier as you go. On the other

hand, the technical aspects of correct walking can be daunting at first. Of course you want to differentiate between the effort and the task. When you are a Bagua Grandmaster you will still be playing with these problems so don't worry too much. Here is some help though: understand the priorities and things will go much better. Here's the basic order; ask yourself these questions:

1. Am I even walking a circle?
2. Does each foot have its own pathway?
3. Is my stride comfortable?
4. Do I feel balanced?

Whew, that's enough. Try to at least be aware of these points first. Maybe devote a whole session to each point in order. If you are even vaguely accomplishing this, give yourself a nice Bagua rest and have some tea. You are "in the circle" of true Bagua practitioners.

Q: Sometimes I forget the order. Is it important?
A: The order of the animals is also taken from the I Ching. It is known as the "Post Heaven" order and represents the order of the eight changes relating to the human in the everyday world. In real practice, the order is not important. However you can fall back on a standard order if, for instance, you don't think you are keeping good track of how many of "these" circles you have done compared to how many of "those" circles, etc. One alternate order which gives a great sense of how each animal differs from its mates is the order of opposites, something like this:

1. Lion and Unicorn: Heaven and Earth
2. Eagle and Snake: Wide and Narrow
3. Phoenix and Monkey: Open and Closed
4. Bear and Sparrow Hawk: Downward and Upward

Q: When do you perform an Inside or Outside Change? Does it matter?
A: It matters a lot. The idea of any Change is to take it spontaneously from where you happen to be on the circle. If your inside leg is forward, your change has to be to the outside. If your outside leg is forward, the reverse is true. The idea is to perform

the change the moment it enters your mind, as though someone attacked and you had to instantly reverse direction. Sometimes you will see people with dance experience, for instance, get out of some tangle on stage by performing, say, a step-over. This does not work for Bagua; every change must be performed with no additional steps. Also, no Change should force your feet to break contact with the ground just to complete the change.

Ted Mancuso began his martial training in 1966. The youngest black belt to graduate from one of the largest schools in the country, he almost immediately became a head instructor for the burgeoning franchise era in martial arts. Meanwhile he kept up his studies of Kung Fu, Tai Chi and Bagua Zhang. After twenty years of training and teaching he opened his first school in Santa Cruz, California. During this period he taught thousands of students, began Plum Publications—a well-known martial arts publishing company—and published two books and hundreds of martial articles in English, Spanish and Chinese. Still teaching from his Santa Cruz school he is originating a series of seminars to bring more martial experiences to a wider audience.

Debbie Shayne has emerged as one of the best martial arts photographers in the country. Her images grace a number of Plum books and have appeared in Inside Kung Fu, Black Belt and other magazines. She is the co-publisher and head buyer for Plum Publications. She employs her wide knowledge of the book business to aid her special interest of "finding and rescuing" martial publications that have gone out of print or have become hard-to-find. She is also the Graphics Editor for all of Plum's own publishing ventures.

If you haven't already done so, please visit us at **www.plumpub.com**, and at our world famous blog, plumpub.com/kaimen. There you will find over 3000 DVDs, VCDs and books on Chinese martial arts, Qigong, self defense, and Asian philosophy.

You will also discover a wealth of **free** information—hundreds of articles, lessons, training tips and reviews—on Kung Fu styles, Tai Chi and Bagua practices, historical background, video tutorials and much more.

Drop by our site, read our blog, leave a comment. Join us in keeping one of the world's great arts alive and thriving.

Of Related Interest...

Tom Bisio's Bagua Neigong

Learning Bagua Zhang:
The Martial Art of Change

Bagua Zhang: The Art of Change
This 2-DVD best-selling series by Ted Mancuso, gives you a complete course in Bagua Zhang.

Adam Hsu's Bagua DVDs
including the 8 Animal "Internal Palms"

And work from other famous Bagua teachers such as: **Liu JingRu, Tony Yang, Deng Fu Ming, Tom Bisio Luo Jin Hua, Sun ZhiJun, Zhu BaoZhen, Luo DeXiu, Park Bok Nam and more...**